The Money Tree

Risk Free Options Trading

D1496360

by

Ronald Groenke

and

Wade Keller

The Money Tree
Risk Free Options Trading

Published by
Keller Publishing
590 Fieldstone Dr.
Marco Island, FL 34145

www.KellerPublishing.com

Dedication

To my lovely wife, Vergeane (Jean), who always gave me encouragement in all my endeavors and has been by my side every step of the way.

RG

To my wife, Suzanne (Sue), our daughters Michelle, Candace, Lily and our grandchildren Joshua, Sarah, Jacob, Josiah, Jonathan.

WK

Disclaimer

There is a high degree of financial risk when trading in the stock and options market. In the title the term "Risk Free Options Trading" means there is no additional risk introduced as a result of selling covered calls.

The authors and publisher stress that it is possible to lose money that is invested in the stock market. The concepts and techniques presented in this book may be profitable or they may result in a loss. Past results are necessarily not indicative of future results. The examples of specific companies that are used in this book are only for informational purposes and are not recommendations.

This publication is sold with the understanding that the authors and publisher are not engaged in providing legal, accounting, or other professional services. If legal advice or other expert assistance is required, the services of a competent professional should be sought. Although every precaution has been taken in the preparation of this book, the publisher and authors assume no liability for errors and omissions. This book is published without warranty of any kind, either expressed or implied. Furthermore, neither the authors nor the publisher shall be liable for any damages, either directly or indirectly arising from the use or misuse of the book.

Before investing, learn as much as you can about the investments that you plan to make. Do extensive research. Knowledge will put the odds in your favor.

Preface

Suppose you have farmland that you have no intention of using or selling in the next few years. Would it make sense to rent it out and generate some income? Or suppose you have some cash under the mattress that you don't need immediately. Would it make sense to put it in a money market account and generate some income? By the same reasoning suppose you have a stock portfolio that you don't intend to sell in the near future. Would it make sense to sell CALL options on some of the stocks and generate income? There is no additional risk. You have already assumed the risk of stock ownership. After selling CALL options, if the stock goes up enough your stock gets called (you sell it) at a price you specified. If the stock stays about the same or goes down, the CALL option expires. In either case you pocket the money (premium) generated by selling the option.

This simple idea is available for anyone to use. The problem is that most investors, even most financial advisors, do not understand the advantage of using options to enhance portfolio performance. If the additional returns on your investment seem unreal after you have implemented some of the strategies in this book, great for you. You keep the rewards of your new investment skills and we have the satisfaction knowing that we were able to advance your financial well being.

Table of Contents

1

"Why not go out on a limb. That's where the fruit is."
Will Rodgers

"Wayne, you're a pain." Sara Kimball smiled at her husband of 30 years. Before selling Kimball CPA Firm and retiring to south Florida, Wayne could be counted on to be out of the house and at the office at least 10 hours a day.

Looking up from the New York Times Book Review with a confused but innocent look Wayne quietly replied, "Yes, dear?" His transgression had been not hearing his wife's question.

"I said, 'Are you going to Rotary today?' And now that I've got your attention would you mind not scattering your newspapers all over the floor. And by the way the Petersons are just back from the Alaska cruise. I saw Lori at Walgreens and she was driving a new BMW convertible. So cute. Their son has graduated from Bowdoin and is accepted at Harvard Law School. Now if you are going to Rotary I will press that new shirt I got for you at Goodwill. But if you are not going we should go walk on the beach because it's low tide now and you know ...."

The phone rang and Wayne quickly retreated again to the safe environment of the book reviews. Before he could find where he had left off the worrisome thoughts came again. He laid the paper down and looked out the window at the areca palms they had planted as a border across the back of their modest home only three blocks from the beach. He had sold the CPA firm too soon and for too little. In their

1

mid fifties they had moved to the pleasant community of Marco Island with plans to write the *Great American Novel* and get it published before their savings ran out. A recent statement from their investment advisor had shown that funds in the retirement account were getting dangerously low. And unless he got the novel finished and published, that was all they had to live on.

These thoughts were never far from his mind. His wife's comments about his new shirt from "Goodwill" and the conspicuous consumption by their friends, Lori and Steve Peterson, had caused his financial concerns to come roaring back to the surface. He needed to do something. Take action. And, by golly, he would. He glanced quickly at his watch. Yep, he concluded decisively, plenty of time for another cup of coffee before going to Rotary.

****

Wayne stood in awe. Like an appreciative artist admiring a Rodin sculpture, he stood looking at the most beautiful Mercedes Benz he had ever seen. Long and powerful, it made a statement of elegant practicality. It had caught his attention as he was about to enter the Olde Marco Inn for the Rotary luncheon. He enjoyed the Marco Island Rotary Club. It was a close-knit, fun group and he knew all the members. Several owned expensive cars. Asa's Rolls Royce came to mind. He was curious wondering which of his friends had acquired the new Mercedes.

The invocation and pledge of allegiance to the flag were followed by introduction of guests. Looking across the room Wayne saw his friend Steve Peterson stand up to

2

introduce a guest who looked vaguely familiar. The visitor reminded him of a college professor from years ago. What was the name? Graham? Yes that was it. Professor Robert Graham. But that's not likely he thought. After all he hadn't seen the professor in over 30 years.

His mind easily slipped back to a particular scene from his college days. He had pulled frantically into the parking lot, already five minutes late for his first class of the semester. It was a hot fall day at the University of Minnesota. As he grabbed his books from the back seat he noticed another car jerk to a stop in the vacant slot next to him. Steam was billowing from under the hood and the car was generally banged up. Wayne noticed the windshield had a long crack. Apparently the driver's side door wouldn't open because the young man slid across the front seat and quickly out the passenger side with brief case in hand.

"Can I help you?" Wayne had asked, concerned that the car might catch on fire.

Noticing Wayne for the first time, the man quickly said, "Hi. Sorry, don't have time to chat. I'm running late for class. Old Betsy will be OK once she cools off. Powerful thirst." With that the man raced into the building

As Wayne made his way to the classroom he was surprised to see the owner of the old clunker standing at the lectern. Finding a seat Wayne noticed the professor had a pleasant smile and twinkle in his eyes as he said to the class, "Welcome to Finance 101. My name is Robert Graham. Don't call me doctor yet as I still have a little work to do on my Ph.D. dissertation. Just call me professor."

"We have a former Rotarian. A Paul Harris Fellow." The sound of Steve Peterson's commanding baritone voice brought Wayne back to the present. "My special guest today has a suite on the same floor at my condominium. We met on the elevator this morning and, spur of the moment, I invited him to join us for lunch. Please give a warm Rotary welcome to a new resident of Marco Island, Dr. Robert Graham."

After the meeting Wayne wasted no time in introducing himself to the professor. "Hi professor. Remember me? Wayne Kimball. I was in your finance class at UM, fall of 1970."

Rob shook hands and smiled as he searched his memory bank. So many students over a twenty-year teaching career. And now he had been retired from teaching for ten plus years.

"Hmmm. You say you were in my class at the University of Minnesota. That was actually my first teaching job. Wait a minute. Were you by chance the student who helped me get my car started after that first class? You had something you poured in the radiator to stop the leak. And then we used a bucket to get water and fill up the radiator."

Wayne was smiling and nodding. "Yes, that was me. It was a good class, Finance 101, but as an accounting major that was the only finance class I needed."

They continued talking as they walked out to the parking lot. Wayne noticed they were heading in the direction of the Mercedes he had admired earlier. His first thought was serious doubt that a former college professor could own such an expensive car. Then he remembered Steve Peterson's comment in introducing Rob. Steve and Lori lived in one of the two penthouse suites on the top floor of one of the most expensive condos on the beach. And Steve had said that Rob lived on the same floor. All of this went through his mind as they continued to talk and were soon standing next to the Mercedes.

4

Wayne's look of amazement was obvious. Rob smiled and said, "This is Old Betsy. A little different from the one you helped me with."

"Professor I don't mean to be nosey but I've got to ask. What did you do, win the lottery?"

"No Wayne, not the lottery. But I guess you could say I discovered a money tree." Rob paused and seemed lost in thought for a moment. Then he noticed that Wayne was waiting patiently for more information, like the good student he had been many years before.

"Wayne it was right under my nose all those years I was teaching finance. About 12 years ago I discovered a way of earning a guaranteed, high rate of return on a stock portfolio with no additional risk. As soon as I knew for sure it was working I retired from teaching and devoted all my time to investing. Say Wayne it's good to see you. I'll probably be joining the club." Rob pulled out his cell phone, pushed a few buttons and the powerful engine purred gently as the driver's side door swung open.

"But professor, wait. What did you mean by "money tree" and "guaranteed high rate of return"? How can I learn more about this?" Wayne hoped he didn't sound desperate.

"Hmmm. Maybe it is about time I became a professor again. Let me make a quick call.

"Hello Jean. I'm going to be about 30 minutes late. I met an old friend at the Rotary meeting. Yes love. I love you too. Meet at the same place, thirty minutes later." Then he reached in his car and retrieved a notebook. "I have an example in here. Let's go back inside and sit down at a table."

When they settled at a secluded table Rob pulled out a sheet of paper, looked at the paper and looked at Wayne.

"Wayne what I am about to show you is very simple and yet very powerful. I've only got time to give you a quick overview right now. I promise we will get together again. In fact maybe I should give you a homework assignment. Here, take a look at an investment I made in K-Mart a while back. I gave myself a blue light special."

The paper contained the following table:

KMART	KM		MAR	JUN	SEP	DEC
11-30-99	B	1000 9.937			9947.50	-9947.50
11-30-99	S	10 MAR 10.00	1.3125		1279.95	-8667.55CE
03-20-00	S	10 SEP 10.00	1.5000		1467.45	-7200.10CE
09-18-00	S	10 MAR 10.00	.9500		917.47	-6282.63CE
03-09-01	S	10 JUN 10.00	1.2500		1217.46	-5065.17CA
06-15-01	C	1000 10.00			9980.66	4915.49

Rob remained silent. After a couple of minutes Wayne looked up.

"Professor, I believe I understand part of the first line. On November 30, 1999 you bought 1000 shares of K-Mart at $9.937 a share. But I'm not sure I understand the last two columns. Where did the 9947.50 come from? And why do the numbers in the last column go from negative to positive?"

"This is my short hand way of keeping up with my investments," explained Rob. "I have developed a software program that analyzes each of my investments as part of my overall portfolio. My primary concern is cash flow. I don't like to lose money. On each investment my first objective is to have a positive cash flow. My second objective is to have a *very* positive cash flow. But more about that later. First let's make sure you understand the basics here.

"You are correct that I bought 1000 shares of K-Mart. The price per share was $9.937. I use a discount, on-line broker and the sales commission was $10.50. Add the sales commission of $10.50 to the purchase of 1000 shares at $9.937 a share and you have my total cash outflow. For this one purchase my total cash outflow was $9,947.50. The next to the last column is the transaction amount and the last column is a running total or the cumulative effect of all the transactions. Since this was a cash outflow the dollar amount is shown as a negative. By the way sales commissions have come down. Today a stock purchase only costs me $5.

"But now let's take a look at the second line of the K-Mart chart. On the same day that I bought the 1000 shares, I sold 10 contracts of March calls at a strike price of $10. The S in the first column means I made a sale. In the next column the "10 MAR 10.00" tells me what I sold. One contract is for 100 shares, the minimum needed to sell an option. So my 1000 shares of stock allow me to sell 10 contracts. That means that at the time the market price of K-Mart was $9.94 a share I sold the option for someone to buy my 1000 shares for $10 a share any time up until the close of the market on the third Friday the following March. $10 is the strike price. If the market price stays at or below $10 it will not be profitable for the buyer of the option to buy my shares for $10. Only if the market price goes above $10 will it be profitable for the option buyer to exercise the option. The price I received for that option was $1.3125 per share. Less commission that came to $1,279.95.

"Notice that the transaction amount, next to last column, is positive. Selling the call means I received money so it is a cash inflow. That has the effect of reducing the cumulative balance in the last column. At this point my net investment is $8,667.55 for the 1000 shares of K-Mart.

"My strategy here is called a covered call. That means I owned the stock, 1000 shares of K-Mart, and on those shares I sold a call option. It's called a "covered" call because, in the event the stock is called, I'm already covered. I already own the stock and can readily hand it over. The purchaser of the option has the right, but not the obligation, to purchase my 1000 shares of K-Mart for $10 a share anytime up to the close of the market on March 17, 2000. I received the premium of $1,279.95 for selling that right or option. Now the purchaser can be expected to exercise the option if the market price of K-Mart goes above $10 during that time period. It could be exercised anytime before expiration but most likely the option would not be exercised until the last day of the option period. Of course it would be foolish to exercise the option if the market price remains below $10.

"As it turned out the call option was not exercised. See the "CE" at the end of line two. CE stands for "Call Expired".

Wayne was beginning to see an entirely new concept in stock ownership. "Hmmmm," he began, "you are actually generating a stream of income just from owning stocks. Do many people do this? I don't think I've heard about it before. I've got a lot of questions. Are there many stocks that you can do this with? What kind of investment return can you make?

8

"Hold on Wayne. First let me ask you a few questions. Maybe it would be best if you told me your impression of the stock market." Rob's professorial techniques were kicking in.

Wayne and Sara had most of their funds invested in the stock market. They were in mutual funds managed by their investment advisor. Wayne thought for a moment before responding.

"Individual stocks go up and down. Over time most of the stocks go up more than they go down so the overall market goes up gradually over time. The market is risky because some stocks go down more than up and may even end up worthless. We have our investments diversified in mutual funds to minimize the risks. That's about all I know. Well I guess I could add what my investment advisor says. His name is Walt Abbott. According to Walt your best strategy is to just sit tight for the long haul. Don't try to time the market. Don't worry about the ups and downs because over the long haul it will be up. And of course, his main advice, *trust Walt* to put us in decent mutual funds."

"That's a pretty good analysis of the market, Wayne. What kind of return, over the long haul, would you expect to achieve with a good mutual fund?"

"Seems like 12% comes to mind. I'm not sure that's right. Maybe that's what the good mutual funds get."

"That's pretty close. One of the people in the investment community who I have a lot of respect for is John Bogle. Bogle pioneered the concept of index funds. These are mutual funds designed to closely mirror the performance of the overall market. Since the objective is to catch the total market performance there is no need to be buying and selling stocks trying to out perform the market. Consequently in

Bogle's funds the administration fees are very low. A surprising finding was that the index funds actually out performed most of the managed mutual funds. The few managed funds that did out perform the index funds couldn't do it on a consistent basis. I only bring up Bogle to cite an analysis of stock market return that he made in one of his books, *"John Bogle on Investing: The First 50 Years"*. For the decade from 1969 to 1979 the annual rate of return on U.S. stocks was 5.8%. However for the two decades from 1979 to 1999 the rate of return was 17.7%. That return for those two decades was the highest ever for the 200 year history of the stock market. Stock prices were basically doubling every four years. You might want to ask Walt if the return on his mutual funds did as well as index funds.

"Here's my pocket calculator and your first test for this semester. What was my return on investment from selling those ten call contracts? By the way one contract is for 100 shares of stock."

Wayne eagerly took the calculator and began solving the problem. He decided that the return for selling the call was $1,279.95. Now what should be the investment base to divide into the return? Well apparently the total cash outflow of $9,947.50. Dividing the former by the later he got 12.86%. He started to state the answer but then the thought occurred: over what time period. He smelled a trap. Sure, 12.86% was a good return but that was for less than a year. What was the APR, annual percentage rate? How many days from November 30, 1999 to March 20, 2000? A quick count gave him 111 days. So to annualize the return he multiplied 12.86 by 365 and divided by 111.

Looking at the professor he said, "42.28% sir."

"Very good Wayne. Actually I never bother to annualize. I have another technique that I'll tell you about

10

later. I'm satisfied with a good, quick return. Just for the heck of it why don't you compute the return for line three."

Wayne quickly noted that the premium per share for the next sell of ten call contracts was $1.50 per share. After commissions Rob had netted $1,467.45. Now what was the amount of investment at that time? Presumably $8,667.53. He quickly made the computation.

"I get 16.93% without annualizing. However annualizing would be fairly simple. It took six months to earn the 16.93%. So just double it for the APR. Either way it's a darn good return."

"Very good. Now here's another question for you. Most investment advisors say the way to make money in the stock market is to buy good stocks and hold for long-term appreciation. Or, as John Bogle would say, buy the whole market and hold for the long term. How much of my return on K-Mart was a result of stock appreciation or dividends?"

Wayne knew better than to make a snap response. He looked closely at the chart again.

"Professor you told me that CE stands for Call Expired. What does CA stand for?"

"CA stands for Call Assigned. That means that on June 15, 2001 the market price of K-Mart was above $10 a share and the owners of the call option exercised their rights. They bought my 1000 shares for $10 a share. My 1000 shares were assigned to the option holders."

"Then the answer is that a small portion of your gains was due to stock appreciation. I guess you got about 6.3 cents a share. But that was really a small part of your over all return. Almost all of your return was from selling the call options. Apparently none of your return was from dividends."

"That's right," said Rob. "There are a couple of very important lessons to draw from the K-Mart experience. You probably know that K-Mart recently filed for bankruptcy protection and its shares were selling for less than $1. An important aspect of the money tree strategy is that we are more interested in the fruit than in the tree. The fruit is "for sure". The tree may not be, especially in the long run.

"In the K-Mart example I sold calls four times, or pulled fruit from the tree four times. Then I was finished with that particular tree and moved on."

"But wait a minute," Wayne exclaimed. "What if your timing had not been so good. What if you are picking fruit as the price of the stock is headed down?"

"Good point. And it can happen. In fact I think I have another example here that illustrates just that experience." Rob pulled a sheet of paper out of his note book and handed it to Wayne. "Cott Corporation is a soft drink bottler. You can see that its stock price went from $9.50 a share down to $3.81 a share. During that time I picked so much fruit from the tree I made a profit of $9,847.80 even though I finally sold the stock at a loss.

"There is a definite risk in owning stock," Rob continued. "But that risk can be greatly mitigated, and in some cases even overcome, by selling calls. This particular investment reminds me of a small town in Minnesota. Have you ever heard of the town of Andover?"

Wayne's head was reeling as he was still analyzing the sheet of paper detailing Rob's investment in Cott. He was counting the number of times calls had been sold on this one

COTT CORPORATION CQT FEB MAY AUG NOV					
11-08-94 B	1500 9.500			-14279.00	-14279.00
11-08-94 S	15 MAY 10.000	1.5625	2298.67	-11980.33	CE
11-30-94 B	1500 10.000			-15029.00	-27009.33
11-30-94 S	15 MAY 10.00	1.7500	2579.91	-24429.42	CE
02-09-95 B	2000 9.625			-19279.00	-43708.42
02-09-95 S	20 AUG 10.00	1.3750	2694.90	-41013.52	CE
05-22-95 S	30 NOV 10.000	.9375	2742.40	-38271.12	CE
08-22-95 S	20 NOV 10.000	.6250	1199.95	-37071.17	CE
11-15-95 S	50 MAY 10.000	.6250	3024.89	-34046.28	CE
05-20-96 S	50 NOV 10.000	.7500	3649.87	-30396.41	CE
11-18-96 S	50 MAY 10.000	.4375	2087.42	-28308.99	CE
05-19-97 S	50 AUG 10.000	.6250	3024.89	-25284.10	CE
08-18-97 S	20 NOV 10.000	.6250	1199.95	-24084.15	CE
08-18-97 S	30 NOV 10.000	.5625	1637.44	-22446.71	CE
11-24-97 S	50 FEB 10.000	.7500	3649.87	-18796.84	CE
02-24-98 S	50 MAY 10.000	.6250	3024.89	-15771.95	CE
05-15-98 S	50 AUG 7.500	.5000	2397.41	-13374.54	CE
08-25-98 S	50 NOV 7.500	.5000	2397.41	-10977.13	CE
11-17-98 S	50 MAY 7.500	.3750	1772.43	-9204.70	CE
06-23-99 S	5000	3.812	19052.50	9847.80	

investment. He just managed to look up and mumble, "No, don't think so."

"The story of how the town got its name is interesting. The Great Northern Railroad had a stop at a small northern town in the late nineteen twenties. One morning there was a derailment and the train rolled over and over and over. This accident was such a big news story the residents decided to rename the town to Andover, to capture the event forever in history. I'm reminded of the name, Andover, when I sell calls over and over."

Wayne was still full of questions as Rob's phone rang. "Yes Jean. I'm on the way. I'll see you in 10 minutes."

Looking at Wayne he said, "Good thing this is a small island. OK you've learned a lot. Now here's your homework assignment. Get a copy of the Wall Street Journal. Go to the options page and pick three stocks that you are familiar with. I want you to assume a purchase of 100 shares of stock and sale of one covered call contract. Pick an option where the strike price - that is the price for which you are committed to sell - is close to the market price. Don't worry this will all become clear when you do the exercise. Remember once you've bought the stock you have assumed the risk of stock ownership. What you are doing by selling calls is generating income. I call it "picking dollars off the money tree". You should be taking notes by the way.

"Here's a sheet of paper. Let's start over. First go to the options page of the Wall Street Journal. Your local paper may also have an options page. You might find prices for both calls and puts. Let's not talk about puts. Just concentrate on calls. Pick three stocks. Now for each stock pick four call option contracts. Notice how the first K-Mart option I sold was designated. It reads March 10.00. That means the strike price is $10 and expiration is the third Friday in March.

Options always expire at the close of business on the third Friday of the month. I suggest you select for analysis four different call option contracts for each stock. Using K-Mart again as an example, I sold March 10. Others that I considered were March 12.50, June 10 and June 12.50. Do you see what I am saying? Look at options from the standpoint both of strike price and expiration date. Since we are considering two strike prices and two expiration dates we have four possible combinations. Now compute the return for each of the four contracts assuming first CE and then CA. Those are the only two things that can happen. Either the call will expire, CE, or the call will be assigned, CA. Compute your return both ways. You will be making a total of 12 computations, four for each of the three stocks.

"You might as well write down the formulas for computing the return. They are:

If Sold =	$\dfrac{\text{(Strike Price + Premium - Purchase Price)}}{\text{Purchase Price}}$
If Expired =	$\dfrac{\text{Premium}}{\text{Purchase Price}}$

"You'll be surprised how much you learn just doing this exercise."

Wayne was writing furiously on the sheet of paper. He looked up to see the professor headed for the door.

"Professor, I've got questions. And when will you check my homework?"

Rob's phone rang before he got to the door. Pulling out the phone and looking over his shoulder at Wayne he said, "I'll come back to Rotary next week. See you then."

And he was gone.

2

"If a man points at the moon, an idiot will look at the finger." Sufi Saying

"Sara my love, you are not going to believe who I met at Rotary today." Wayne arrived home in a state of excitement with his newly purchased copy of the Wall Street Journal.

"Let me guess," replied Sara with a sly smile. "Could it possibly have been Rob Graham, the Finance Professor you had in college?" As Wayne's mouth hung open she continued. "I've just been on the phone with Lori. Steve is rather perturbed with you. He says you shanghaied his guest before he could introduce him to the membership chair and the president. According to Lori the only way we can make up for your outrageous indiscretion is for us to come over for cocktails and sunset on their balcony. So I accepted. Is that alright?"

"Sure. You know I'm always glad to visit with Steve and Lori. Besides I need to pick Steve's brain. He retired near the top of that big brokerage firm. With all the money they have he must have done really well as a stockbroker, or analyst, whatever he was. But right now I've got homework to do. I'm computing how much money we can make by selling covered calls."

"Covered who? Oh never mind. Just let me know when I can read another chapter of your novel. I'm anxious to find out how your "Walter Mitty" CPA character saves the nation from financial ruin."

17

As Wayne did his computations he became increasingly familiar with the operations of the options market. Several points became obvious. Apparently there were three factors in his decision process which determined the amount of premium he could receive by selling a call option.

First, the time period to the expiration date was important. The premium offered for one month was not as great as the premium offered for three months or six months. The longer the option was in effect the more it was worth. He also noticed the "time value" of money come into play. A six month option, while more than a three month option, was less than twice the value; a three month option, worth more than a one month option, was less than three times the value.

The second factor under his control was the selection of the strike price. If a stock were selling for $12.50, a strike price of $15 would pay less than a strike price of $10. That made sense because with a $15 strike price the stock would have to rise more than $2.50 before the option would be exercised. A strike price of $10 meant the stock was already $2.50 above the price at which it could be bought by the option holder. A strike price of $10 meant the option already had $2.50 of intrinsic value in addition to its time value.

The third factor was the particular stock that he selected. Wayne found two stocks that had the same closing price the previous day. When he checked the option premium for each, using the same strike price and expiration date, he found that stock A would yield a significantly higher premium than stock B. Maybe that had something to do with the volatility of the stock. That would bear checking out.

He began to formulate some questions for the professor. First how do you know which stocks to buy? Is it just random or is there a way to wisely select stocks? Second how do you know which strike price and time period to choose? He began to suspect that once he had those questions answered there would be more questions. He was deep in thought when Sara came over and pulled on his ear lobe.

"Let's go for a walk, handsome, and you can tell me how much money we are going to make with that covered stuff. We'll need to get back in plenty of time to make sunset with Steve and Lori."

****

"Wayne, I'll bet you were surprised to see Rob. I had no idea you two knew each other." Wayne and Sara had enjoyed a vigorous walk on the beach, showered and changed before going to the Peterson's penthouse condo for sunset and cocktails. Steve was in a bombastic mood. He had already extolled the virtues of his favorite sports teams and denigrated the lack of virtue of certain local political figures.

"Yes", Wayne replied. "I was very pleasantly surprised. Rob Graham was my Finance Professor over thirty years ago. He had a certain presence in the classroom, you might say charisma, that makes him easy to remember."

"You'll notice," Steve interrupted because this was his favorite time of day, "that the bottom of the sun has just touched the Gulf of Mexico. It will be exactly two minutes and forty six seconds until the sun is completely down. And I would say the conditions are good for a green flash this evening. Humidity is low and there are only a few clouds near the horizon."

The green flash was a popular topic of conversation. It occurred rarely and would only happen when the last of the sun dipped into the sea. Perhaps one time in a hundred a

19

green flash could be seen just at that moment of last sunlight. You could consider yourself lucky if you saw it once. But of course the Petersons had seen it numerous times with their front row seat.

"Speaking of green," Wayne piped in, "what do you think of making money in the options market?"

"You will lose your shirt," Steve replied with conviction. "You might as well go to Vegas and play the crap table. In my thirty years on Wall Street I never knew anyone to consistently make money buying options. It's just a gamble."

"Steve I never did understand exactly what you did on Wall Street."

"I started off as a broker. And then I managed one of our branch offices with about 50 brokers. So we were basically in sales. I would have clients occasionally who would insist on playing the options market. After they lost all they could afford I would then get them into some good solid companies for long term growth. I tell you, people who think they can manage their own money in the stock market, why that's like trying to operate on yourself. There are some things that just need to be handled by professionals and the stock market is one of them. My clients over the years would just turn every thing over to me. They didn't want to be bothered with the decisions. And of course my job was to preserve their capital. I guess you could say my motto was 'preserve and grow slowly'. And it paid off. We've been retired for fifteen years now, enjoying the good life. You know the old 80-20 rule. Well that applied with my clients. 80% of my problems came from the 20% who were always coming up with a hot stock tip or strategy, like the ones that wanted to gamble in the options market. I would give those clients to new trainees and keep the satisfied clients. All brokers like clients who appreciate their knowledge and expertise. Leave the driving to us, so to speak."

Steve leaned back in the lounge chair and smiled contentedly, enjoying the warm breeze, commanding view of the beach and the gulf. Four pelicans gracefully flew by. There were sailboats in the distance. The clouds were just right to pick up a red tint from the sun.

"But what if, Steve, instead of buying options, you sold options. And suppose further that you only sold options on stock that you already owned. Would that not be risk free income?"

Steve was about to take a sip of his margarita, Lori's specialty. Lori liked to brag that she had learned the secret recipe after chatting with the bartender at a local Mexican restaurant. The glass had reached Steve's lips and seemed to be frozen there. Time stood still. Finally Steve set the glass down and absent-mindedly licked the salt off his lips. His voice was usually a little on the loud side. But now it was low, just barely audible. He seemed almost to be talking to himself. "Hmmm. Sell options on stock that you own. Yes that would seem to work. Maybe that's why so many people buying options lose money. It's because people selling options are making money. If the stock goes up above the strike price you sell at a profit. You get the premium and part of the stock appreciation. If the stock goes down you still keep the premium. Psychologically you are not that concerned that the stock go up right away. Long term sure you want it to go up and, if you pick a good stock, it will. But if the stock goes down you could buy the option back for pennies on the dollar and sell it again when the stock goes back up. Or just wait for the option to expire and then sell a new contract on the same stock. What's the risk? Well the stock price could move up sharply and your gain on the up side would be limited. But that rarely happens. Stocks move

21

up over time but over short periods like three months, they mostly just move up and down within a narrow range. Of course the real risk is that the stock could go down. But you have that risk whether you sell options or not. So if you mean by 'risk free income' no additional risk then ......"

Steve interrupted his rambling monologue and shouted to Lori, "Honey, would you bring me the Wall Street Journal." And then to Wayne, "I wonder what kind of premium I could get on my portfolio? Why you know the more I think about it the more obvious it is. Hardly any stocks pay a decent dividend any more. The portfolio is just sitting there. And I'm sitting here hoping the market will go up a little bit. I've got dozens of stocks that have been virtually flat over the past couple of years. Might as well generate a little income while they're sitting there. Wayne let me fix you another drink. Lori, did you throw out the papers?"

Wayne noticed that the sky had become even more beautiful after the sunset. He smiled, looking forward to his next meeting with the professor.

3

"You should invest in companies that even a fool can run, because someday a fool will."   Warren Buffett

"Wayne I am truly impressed. That was exactly the right question to ask. I seem to remember that you made an A in that Finance 101 class."

Wayne laughed. "No not exactly professor. I had an A going into the final. But then I got distracted toward the end of the semester. Her name is Sara. I would like for you to meet her. We've been blessed with three daughters and five grandkids."

Wayne and Rob were again at their secluded table at the Olde Marco Inn. The Rotary Club meeting had ended and Wayne had waited patiently as Rob met the Membership Chairman and filled out the paperwork to be proposed for membership. As they settled down at their table Rob ordered a cup of herbal tea and Wayne asked, "How do I know which stocks to buy?"

Rob continued. "You've no doubt heard the term *Buy Low ~ Sell High*. It's such a popular statement that it's become a cliché, you might say flippant. But nevertheless that is the fundamental strategy for buying stocks."

Rob paused for a sip of tea and Wayne interjected. "But professor that's easy to say. Buy Low. Sure but how do you know you are at the low point. The price could just keep going down?"

"That's true. There are no guarantees. But if you are interested I will give you my strategy for buying low and selling high."

The professor paused again, gathering his thoughts. Wayne decided he should talk less and listen more, so he just nodded agreement and with pen in hand adjusted the note pad on the table. He put the date at the top and wrote, "Buy Low Sell High".

Rob continued. "Anyone can succeed if the stocks that are picked go up and all transactions are at a gain. I have however developed some stock selection principles and techniques that have proven very effective. Seems like every time I deviate from them I get burned.

"My first principle is this: ***Search for good companies with options. Build a qualified prospect list.***

"You have to search for good companies since they are not obvious. You should first look in an industry or market that you are familiar with. No matter what your background is, you probably can name thirty to fifty companies very quickly that touched your life in the last twenty-four hours one way or another. From the cereal you had for breakfast, the type of vehicle you drive, the brand of gas you use, the last store you shopped, to the computer on your desk, there are various companies that could have filled your needs. You picked certain ones because of a fuzzy feeling for the product or good advertising on the company's part. I like the computer and communications networking business. I therefore have a prospect list that is weighted heavily in the computer systems, software, networking, and semiconductor markets. I have supplemented this list with companies in the retail, defense, medical technology, and air transportation areas.

"Identify several marketplace or technology areas that you like and understand. There are a number of places to find these candidates. I always consider stocks that are in the highest volume of shares traded for the day as prospects. High volume is important for two reasons. First you want to always have a market for your stocks. High volume indicates high liquidity. Second, high volume indicates that the market has scrutinized the company very closely. When the market focuses intently on a company, all information available is reflected in the price of the stock. You can then conclude that the stock is accurately priced by the market. No hidden surprises are likely. Look also at the percent gainers and losers list for the day. Check the news. Why did a particular stock go up or down so much in one day? Maybe an analyst upgraded or downgraded the stock, the company beat or missed their earnings estimate, there is new competition, there is a take over rumor or the rumor has been dispelled, etc. There are many reasons. Something major happened and in many cases it is temporary so this may be an opportunity worth tracking.

"I also have found many prospects by looking at the major markets daily and weekly new low lists. Every company has a 52-week high and low. Stocks do go up and down. When good companies hit a new low this is the time to place them on your prospect list and start tracking them. At some point they will move up from this new low and that may be the time we want to get in. We want to buy low and sell calls as the stock moves up. All of this information is available in the Wall Street Journal.

"Now you can narrow down your list to the top three or four prospects in each area by applying the following criteria. Criteria number one, of course, there must be an options market in that company's stock. Not all stocks have options associated with them."

Wayne interjected a quick question. "Professor that reminds me. I meant to ask about indexes. You remember last week you seemed to be saying that someone investing in the stock market would do well to consider index funds. Would that be good for options too?"

"As a general rule I don't sell calls on index funds. You can but the reason not to is they are less volatile than the individual stocks. Volatility is a factor in determining the amount of premium you receive for selling a call. Our objective with selling covered calls is to earn a high return for owning the stock portfolio. The increase in value of the portfolio is important, but secondary to generating a high return. With a high return from selling calls you can buy additional stock and get the compounding effect going. Okay?"

"Yes. I'm beginning to see that."

"Good. Let's recap where we are. In selecting stocks, our overall principal is to "Buy Low, Sell High". So we are going through a process to develop a list of prospects. I recommend that you first consider companies that you are familiar with, companies whose products or services you use. Now here are the specific requirements, qualifiers that a company must meet before I include it in my prospect list:

"Revenue or sales of at least $250 million per year.

"Growth of Revenue over the past 5 years of at least 15% per year.

"Positive earnings, that is net income rather than net loss, in at least three of the last four quarters.

"And finally apply a liquidity test. The stock must trade an average volume of at least 200,000 shares per day.

"Remember, at this point we are simply building a qualified prospect list and organizing it into marketplace or technology areas with three or four companies in each area. We are like the owner of a major league baseball team. We want a lot of players on the farm team. And of course we want to develop player-prospects for each position."

Rob pulled a sheet of paper out of his notebook and handed it to Wayne.

"Here's a list of thirty stocks on my prospect list which I have arranged in ten groups of three. You will need to form your own list based on your particular interests and field of expertise. The next step involves some computations, so be prepared to write down two formulas in just a minute. Maybe before we get to the formulas I should ask you if you have any questions?"

Wayne had a nervous habit of doodling when he was excited and focused. At that moment he was circling the heading on his legal pad - Buy Low ~ Sell High - with small dollar signs. He knew he was on the verge of receiving some very valuable information.

"Well let me see if I understand so far. We are going to generate income by selling calls on stock that we own. That's referred to as covered calls. Step one is to buy good stocks on which to sell the calls. You have a prospect list of 30 stocks. Now we are going to prioritize the list so we know which stocks to buy."

Wayne paused and the professor finished his line of reasoning. "You're right. But remember our objective is to buy low and sell high. That's the proper stock market strategy whether you sell options or not. Once we buy low we then sell a call option with a strike price higher than the market price because we expect the stock to go up. Our plan

ROB GRAHAM PROSPECT LIST

WalMart (WMT)	Oracle (ORCL)
K-Mart (KM)	Microsoft(MSFT)
Target (TGT)	Siebel Systems (SEBL)
Intel (INTC)	Barnes and Nobel (BKS)
AdvMicroDevices (AMD)	BordersGroup (BGP)
Micron Technology (MU)	Amazon.com (AMZN)
Best Buy (BBY)	Cisco Systems (CSCO)
Radio Shack (RSH)	Lucent (LU)
Circuit City (CC)	Motorola (MOT)
Lockheed Martin (LMT)	Sun Micro (SUNW)
General Dynamics (GD)	Hewlett Packard (HWP)
Honeywell (HON)	IBM Corp (IBM)
NorthwestAirlines(NWAC)	Cardinal Health (CAH)
Southwest Airlines (LUV)	Boston Scientific (BSX)
British Air (BAB)	Medtronic (MDT)

is to make money both from the option premium and stock appreciation."

Rob paused again to make sure Wayne was ready to proceed. "OK professor. I'm with you."

"The formulas I will give you are to compute what I call Buy Limit and Buy Rank. These two values allow me very quickly to filter my prospect list and rank the stocks. For every stock you can get its lowest price of the past 52 weeks and its highest price. Let L stand for the 52 week low and H stand for the 52 week high. The Buy Limit formula is as follows:

$$\boxed{\text{Buy Limit} = L + .25(H - L)}$$

"Ideally we would like to buy at L, the 52 week low. But we have to accept the fact that we cannot time the market and know that today's L will not be superseded by an even lower L tomorrow. But it is possible we can catch the stock on the way up from L. That's our objective here. The magic increment is .25(H - L). For example if a stock has a 52 week low of \$10 and a 52 week high of \$40 then the magic increment is \$7.50. That's computed by taking 25% of \$40 minus \$10. You might think of 7.50 as our window of opportunity. I would be interested in buying the stock in the price range from \$10 to \$17.50. As we get closer to \$17.50, the *Buy Limit*, I begin losing interest in the stock. At \$17.50 it is too high. It's easy to see the trend when you are looking at a chart of the stock's prices. I'll show you one in just a moment.

"Now we use the Buy Limit in the following formula to compute the Buy Rank for each stock. Let's let BL stand for Buy Limit and CP stand for the Current Price of the stock. Notice that the denominator is the magic increment we computed to use in the last formula.

$$\text{Buy Rank} = \frac{10(BL - CP)}{.25(H - L)}$$

"When the current stock price is the same as the 52 week low the buy rank is 10. This is its maximum value. When the current stock price is the same as the 52 week high, the buy rank is negative 30. Our Buy Rank formula gives us a range of values on a scale from negative 30 to positive 10."

Rob took Wayne's pen and drew a line on the note pad.

-30   0   +5   ↓ +10

"A stock captures my attention with a Buy Rank between 10 and 5, moving down. A decreasing value in the Buy Rank indicates the stock is moving up in price and perhaps has started its next major up trend.

"For example using our example of a stock with 52 week low of $10 and 52 week high of $40, we computed the Buy Limit to be $17.50. Suppose the current price were $12. At that price we are well below our Buy Limit of $17.50. What is the Buy Rank? It is 10(17.50 - 12) which is 55 divided by 7.50. That's a Buy Rank of 7.33. As the current

30

price rises closer to the Buy Limit the Buy Rank declines, approaching zero. For example a current price of $16 gives a Buy Rank of 2. A current price of $17 gives a Buy Rank of 0.66. And of course a current price of $17.50, the same as the Buy Limit, would give a Buy Rank of zero. So we are only interested in stocks with a positive Buy Rank.

"Let's take a look at a real world example. One of the companies on my prospect list is Siebel Systems (SEBL). It is a provider of eBusiness applications, enabling organizations to sell to, market to, and service their customers across multiple channels. It was on the NASDAQ new low list on 9-29-01. To do my analysis I needed some pertinent information about the stock. There are many places on the internet that provide this information for free. One favorite is www.cbs.marketwatch.com. Enter a stock symbol and then go to "Profile" for the following information.

The key points of information are as follows:

~SEBL stock price 17.22

~52-week high - 119.87

~52-week low - 12.24

~Revenue of over 1.7 Billion per year.

~Sales growth of 120% for the year.

~Earnings were positive the past five quarters.

~Average number of shares traded per day of over fifteen million shares.

First I compute the Buy Limit with the formula
BL = L + .25(H - L)

31

BL = 12.24 + .25(119.87 - 12.24)

That becomes 12.24 + 26.91 or 39.15. Notice that my window of opportunity is 26.91 which is the spread from the low of $12.24 up to the Buy Limit of $39.15. We'll use this figure again in the denominator of the Buy Rank formula.

Next I compute the Buy Rank.

BR = 10(39.15 - 17.22) divided by 26.91

That gives me a Buy Rank of 8.14, a nice positive number between 5 and 10.

"Well, Wayne, what do you think of Siebel as a prospect"?

Wayne had been taking careful notes and decided to review his notes as he responded.

"I wrote down the criteria you require for stocks on your prospect list.

"Sales at least $250 million per year.

"Sales growth at least 15%

"Positive earnings at least three of the last four quarters.

"An average volume of at least 200,000 shares per day.

"Based on what you just told me about Siebel it meets all those criteria and then some. It seems to be a very solid company. I can see that it is important to be sure the company qualifies on those points. If not you might wind up

32

with some real junk. By requiring positive earnings you avoid all the internet stocks that were soaring in price while running up big operating losses."

"That's right Wayne. The typical "dot coms" in the recent internet bubble failed to have positive earnings. And they would also fail my Buy Limit and Buy Rank test. They were usually trading close to a fifty two week high. But meeting my criteria is no guarantee that the stock will go up. What we are really doing is getting the odds on our side. If a company has good sales growth, positive earnings and high liquidity then the odds are it has a bright future. But remember, there are no guarantees. I've been burned several times with what I thought were good companies. However any loss that I incurred because the stock went down was cushioned by the premiums I garnered by selling calls.

"There are basically two reasons to be very careful with stock selection. And these are not the typical reasons you would hear from the average investor or market analyst for that matter. Most investors are trying to buy the right stocks for price appreciation. Frankly I think that's just too difficult for anyone to do on a consistent long term basis. The two reasons I want stocks likely to go up are: 1) Avoid losses and 2) The option premiums are higher if the market has positive expectations for the stock. My return on selling options is so good that I don't really need stock appreciation. What I'm doing is playing good defense as I consistently pick money off the money tree.

"Now I have something else for you to consider. You've heard the saying "A picture is worth a 1000 words'. Well in the case of investing, a picture can be worth thousands of dollars."

With that Rob pulled a chart out of his folder and slid it across the table to Wayne. "Take a look at this."

As Wayne studied the chart Rob walked over to the waiter's station and replenished his cup of herbal tea. As he was pouring the steaming hot water on the tea bag his phone rang.

"Rob, he's here. I just buzzed him in. He's on the way up." Jean's normally calm voice had a tinge of excitement to it.

"Greg?"

He heard the doorbell ring. "Yes dear, it's Greg."

4

"Hope deferred makes the heart sick, but when dreams come true at last, there is life and joy." Proverbs 13:12

"Wayne I'm got about twenty minutes, then I need to go. Let's see. Oh yes, we were going over my Siebel Systems investment. We looked at the Buy Rank and my criteria for sales, earnings and liquidity. At this point Siebel has met all my requirements. The next major concern is the amount of premium I could receive by selling covered calls. I decide to check this out by going to a web site that shows a detailed list of options with bid prices. A site I like to use is www.wallstreetcity.com. On September 29, 2001 here were the quoted call option premiums I checked and the computed gain for "If sold" and "If expired".

Rob handed Wayne the following chart:

Siebel Systems SEBL: FEB MAY AUG NOV			
Month/Strike	**Bid**	**%If Sold**	**% If Expired**
Nov 17.50	2.20	.14	.13
Jan 17.50	3.20	.20	.18
Feb 17.50	3.70	.23	.21
May 17.50	4.60	.28	.26

"The option premiums available are excellent. This was as of September 29, 2001, the day I noticed that Siebel had a Buy Rank of 8.14. Now take another look at the chart I showed you a few minutes ago. It's a 52-week chart of the stock price. Each point represents the daily closing stock price. The smooth line is the fifty day moving average.

Wayne studied the chart closely.

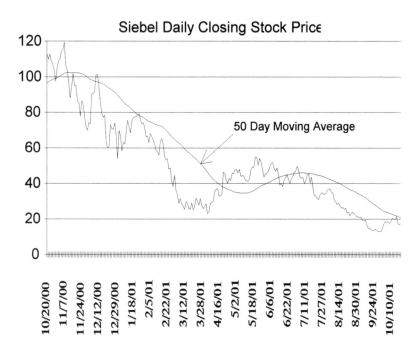

"What's the significance," he asked, "of the fifty day moving average?"

"I like to get the very best odds I can," Rob explained. "I've found that it's not enough to have a stock with a good Buy Rank and good return for selling calls. Those are both critically important. But I want to be as sure as possible that the stock has actually started another up trend. So before investing I look at a picture of the stock. I want to see the current price pass through the fifty day moving average. As long as the current price is leading the average down, don't invest. But when the price breaks above the fifty day moving average, I feel encouraged that we have begun an up trend. Does that make sense?"

"Yes." Wayne was still studying the chart. "I'm surprised that the stock was so high and then went so low. And it looks like the price is still below the fifty day moving average, but very likely to cross it soon."

"Right Wayne. You mentioned the high price of Siebel back in the last quarter of 2000. I like to take out extremes in my calculations. So I decided to use the more recent high figure of 56 in early 2001. This I believe will give a truer picture of where the stock is likely to go in the future. I recomputed the Buy Rank and got a still very respectable 5.45. Each point represents the daily closing stock price for Siebel. Everything looks good except the price is still below the moving average. While the price at 17.22 is above the 52 week low I'm not confident the stock has started an up trend. With a Buy Limit of 23.18 I decided I had plenty of time to catch the stock on the up trend if indeed it did pass the fifty day moving average. I continued following the stock.

"Finally on October 17, 2001 with a price of 16.55 the stock crossed the fifty day moving average. You know how to read these tables. Here's what happened." Rob handed Wayne a sheet of paper with the following chart:

SIEBEL SYSTEMS SEBL			FEB	MAY	AUG	NOV
10-17-01 B	1000 16.55				-16555.00	-16555.00
10-17-01 S	10 Nov 17.50	2.1000			2074.91	-14480.09

Wayne picked up the sheet of paper like it was a rare and valuable document. He studied it intently. Then he took out his pocket calculator and divided $2,074.91 by $16,555.00.

Looking up he quietly said, "Professor I assume you realize you've earned a return of 12.5% on your investment for one month. That's an APR, annual percentage rate, of 150%. And that's assuming the stock is not called. If it is above $17.50 on November 16 your gain will be even more."

"That's true Wayne. But don't forget the stock could go down. That's a risk inherent in owning stock.   Also your APR calculation assumes I can do this each month for a year. There is no guarantee of that. What I'm looking at is my stock may get called on November 16. If so I will have a gain of $3000 on my investment. That will more than pay for our trip to Baltimore to have a nice Thanksgiving with the family. If the stock does not get called I will sell February calls and pick some more money off the tree for Christmas."

"But professor. I mean for crying out loud. We're talking 150% gain."

"Calm down Wayne and don't get carried away with percentages. Notice carefully what I've done. This is not a get rich quick scheme and it's not guaranteed to work for everyone all the time. Right now ask yourself what can go wrong. Based on what you know so far, what can go wrong?"

Wayne looked over his notes and took his time. Money for selling the call was received immediately so that was secure. But what about the investment itself. What if that went down in value.

"There is a risk," Wayne replied, "that the investment could go down. There is always that risk when you are dealing in the stock market. I understand that. That's just a risk you take in owning stock."

"That's true," Rob responded. "But the danger here is that the premium you receive from selling calls is so much like an interest payment that I don't want you to make the mistake of thinking the principal investment is as safe as a CD. It's not.

"A prime example of what can happen in the real world is the trade experience I had with ValuJet (VJET). You already guessed it. I owned the stock when one of their planes crashed. Lets review what happened.

"On 05-03-96 I purchased 2000 shares of VJET for $13.50 each and sold December 12.50 calls for a premium of $3.375. A gain of 25% if expired and 19% if called out in seven months. On May 11, 1996 a ValuJet DC9 crashed into the Everglades in Florida with no survivors. The price of the stock was affected when all of ValuJets planes were grounded. Since I had losses built into my plan I took action on 06-18-96 and closed out my call options (bought them back) and sold the stock the next day.

"What started out to be a good trade turned into a sizable loss with zero warning. Tragic and unforeseen events will happen when least expected. Have some built into your plan.

"I do everything I can to protect against stock market surprises. In fact I have losses built into my plan. I'll tell you more about that later. Now I've really got to go. We have a surprise visitor from up north. I would like for you to meet him some time.

"I keep this account summary with me as constant reminder of what can happen"

Rob handed Wayne the following table:

VALUJET	VJET	VJQ	MAR JUN SEP	DEC
05-03-96 B	2000 13.500		27029.00	-27029.00
05-03-96 S	20 DEC 12.500	3.3750	6664.77	-20364.23 CC
06-18-96 B	20 DEC 12.500	.75	1550.00	-21914.23
06-19-96 S	2000 6.625		13221.00	-8693.23

5

"If a man empties his purse into his head, no one can take it away from him. An investment of knowledge always pays the best interest."   Ben Franklin

Wayne arrived home with a fresh copy of the Wall Street Journal. Before rushing out the professor had suggested he build a qualified prospect list of at least 15 companies, which met the criteria for sales, earnings and liquidity. For each company he was to compute the Buy Limit and Buy Rank. Wayne had decided to subscribe to the Journal, especially after noting that book reviews were a common feature.

As he began reading the paper, looking for prospects, he heard Sara on the lanai, talking on the phone. She was wearing the headset he had given her for her birthday and fussing over the potted plants as she talked. Noticing Wayne she called out, "Pick up the phone Wayne. It's Walt. I've been telling him about the covered stuff."

"Hello Walt. How's the portfolio?"

"That's the reason I called." Wayne noticed that Walt had an unusually somber tone to his voice. Usually he talked a few minutes about the weather in Atlanta and asked about the weather on Marco. "Maybe you both had better sit down. I'm afraid I have some rather bad news."

Sara came inside and they both sat on the couch. "Okay," Wayne said. "We're both sitting down. Let's have it."

"You know I have your funds invested in four mutual funds: large cap growth, small cap growth, large cap value and small cap value." Wayne and Sara were familiar with the introduction. Walt always started off with the importance of diversity and professional management. He would go on to say that while the market was down such and such a percentage as measured by such and such an index, his mutual funds were down a lesser amount. They had played good defense in the down market. They valued Walt's advice and considered him very knowledgeable about the market.

"The bottom line, Wayne and Sara, is that we are not getting the growth or dividends we would need to cover the amount you are withdrawing each month for living expenses. We are in serious danger of the corpus of your funds shrinking to the point that even when the market turns around it will not be able to support the level of withdrawals you require. Would it be possible to reduce your monthly withdrawals to a more sustainable figure? I'm suggesting a one third cut."

Wayne had already gone over their budget during the past few months and knew there was not much opportunity for cuts. As he and Sara silently took in the news, Walt continued.

"I don't recommend transferring to a bond fund. Right now interest rates are at an historical low and can only go up. As rates go up the value of a bond fund goes down. A money market fund would not be susceptible to rate fluctuations but would also not give us enough return. So I think we need to stay with the growth and value fund stocks. There are really no other options."

"Options!" Wayne repeated Walt's last word with emphasis. "What about options, Walt?"

"Oh yes, Sara was telling me you have been studying the options market. I don't really think that's a good idea. There was a buzz about making a good return by selling covered calls a few years back. I think some mutual funds even got into it. But they missed a few sharp rallies in the market and became disillusioned. You've got to remember a stock has a given price which reflects a fine balance between its potential to go up and its potential to go down. Those two forces are balanced at the market price. When you sell a call you are foregoing the upside potential. However you are left with the downside potential. Over the long run you miss gains on the upside and continue to incur the losses on the downside. That exposure to loss, not compensated by upside gains, will more than offset the premium you receive from selling calls."

Wayne's head was reeling. "But what if I always set the strike price higher than the market price. Wouldn't that mean I participate in market rallies?"

"Yes, you can do that," Walt replied. "But remember that the higher the strike price, the price at which someone has the option to buy your stock, the lower the premium you receive. The lower the strike price, i.e. the more of the potential gain you are giving up, the higher the premium. It all balances out."

Wayne felt like he was in over his head and wished the Professor were on the phone to talk to Walt. But nevertheless he dove in. "Walt, you say it all balances out. You make it sound so simple. If all the stocks are fairly priced, that fine balance between up and down, then it doesn't really matter which stocks we invest in. Are you saying that we might as well be in an index fund representing the whole market rather than the four mutual funds you selected?"

"No, no, no. It's not that balanced. Professional management is very important.'

"And do I understand you correctly that the reason not to sell calls is so you participate in market rallies?'

"Yes," Walt replied. "That's right."

"On average how much appreciation could we expect by participating in all the ups and downs of the market?"

"The mutual funds I have you in have averaged about 15% each year since inception. They haven't done that well this year of course. This year the whole market is down."

Wayne thought about the money tree concept. How could he reconcile what he was hearing from Walt with what the professor was telling him? "Walt I hear what you are saying about calls. But do you know anyone who has had success with this strategy?"

"Yes, actually I do, although I think they are forfeiting stock appreciation and could do even better. I'm familiar with a pension fund that needs income to pay pension benefits. They sell calls each month to earn the income for their pensioners."

Up to this point Sara had been quietly listening. "Say fellows," she piped in. "Maybe there are two ways of looking at stock market investments. If you look at it from the standpoint of long term investing everything Walt says makes sense. That way you are committed to the market and only make money when the market goes up. My dad planted acres and acres of pine trees. It was like a twenty year investment for the trees to grow and be cut for pulp wood. That's the long term approach that Walt represents.

"But it seems that selling calls is more like having an orchard. Maybe there are fig trees and orange trees and peach trees in the orchard. And you go through the orchard picking fruit off the trees. You pick fruit in good years and bad years. There's always some fruit available.

"Perhaps you could view the market either way. But whichever way you chose determines how you make money from the market. You know it sort of reminds me of that seminar we went to. Walt we have a friend here – his name is Dan Grant - who is always inviting us to investment seminars. We get a free meal at a nice restaurant. Well this particular one was about equipment leasing. They talked about all the advantages of buying equipment and leasing it out. That's another way of looking at selling calls. We are just buying the stock short term and leasing it out to the people buying our call options. Does that make sense Walt?"

"Yes but….."

Suddenly Wayne had a question. "Walt, let me ask you a question. This is a follow up on what Sara was saying. You said your mutual funds have averaged 15% a year. I imagine some years they have to do a lot better than 15% in order to average 15% overall. Is that right?"

"Yes. We've on occasion had some really good years."

"Okay, here's my questions." Wayne was thinking back to the K-Mart and Seibel examples and the premiums he had computed on his first homework assignment. "Suppose you had to choose between two investments. Investment "A" pays 5% for one month. At the end of one month you can search around for another investment for another month and make another 5%. Investment "B" will average 15% a year provided you hold it for five years. Which investment would you be most interested in?"

"I see your point," Walt replied. "Obviously you intend Investment A to represent selling calls. Can you really make 5% return for one month?"

"Check it out Walt. You might be surprised. Sara and I need to talk this over. But I think we will be calling you back. We may decide to manage our portfolio ourselves."

6

"Invest in companies, not stocks"..... Peter Lynch

After talking to Walt, Wayne was more motivated that ever to learn everything he could about the professor's options strategy. He knew the professor had a lot more to teach him, but he also knew the importance of getting the basics down. So he very dutifully went about his homework assignment, building a qualified prospect list of thirty stocks. For each stock he computed the Buy Limit and Buy Rank using the formulas the professor had given him.

$$\text{Buy Limit} = L + .25(H - L)$$

$$\text{Buy Rank} = \frac{10(BL - CP)}{.25(H - L)}$$

For each stock with a positive Buy Rank, i.e. between zero and 10, Wayne went to www.wallstreetcity.com to find the bid price for selling calls. He organized his call premiums based on the chart the professor had given him illustrating calls on Siebel Systems. That's when a major question arose: which month and strike price was the best? Looking at the chart the professor used for Siebels Systems did not seem to quickly answer the question.

Siebel Systems SEBL: FEB MAY AUG NOV			
Month/Strike	Bid	%If Sold	% If Expired
Nov 17.50	2.20	.14	.13
Jan 17.50	3.20	.20	.18
Feb 17.50	3.70	.23	.21
May 17.50	4.60	.28	.26

"Sara, would you come look at this?" Sara sat down with Wayne and looked at the Siebel calls. Wayne explained what he understood. "The professor used this table to analyze the return he could receive from selling calls on Siebel stock. At the time he did the computation the stock was selling for $17.22 per share. The first row means that the buyer of the call will pay $2.20 a share immediately for the right to buy Siebel for $17.50 anytime up to the close of the market on the third Friday in November. That's November 16th so the time period is just under one month."

"Hold on now. Let me be sure I understand this." Sara followed the line across to .14 and .13. "Does this mean that return on the investment will be either 14% or 13%? Why is there a difference?

The question hearkened back to Wayne's first homework assignment. He wrote down the two formulas and explained the difference.

If Sold =	$$\frac{(\text{Strike Price} + \text{Premium} - \text{Purchase Price})}{\text{Purchase Price}}$$
If Expire =	$$\frac{\text{Premium}}{\text{Purchase Price}}.$$

"The professor gets to keep the premium, whichever premium he decides on, whether the stock is called or not. So to compute the gain if the call expired, meaning the stock is not called by the option holder, simply divide the premium by the purchase price. For example for February calls it would be $3,700 divided by $17,220." Using his calculator Wayne showed Sara the answer of 21.4%.

"Let's compute the gain "If Sold" for the January calls. That would be $17,500 plus $3,200 minus $17,220, which is $3,480. Then divide that by the purchase price of $17,220 and we get 20%."

"Okay," Sara said, "I see the difference. If the stock is called you have to take into account the difference between the strike price and the purchase price. Since the strike price is more that the purchase price you make additional money."

"Right. Now let me show you our prospect list so far. I've computed Buy Limit and Buy Rank for each stock."

Wayne started explaining Buy Limit and Buy Rank. "The Buy Limit is the maximum price we would pay for a stock. When you see that the Buy Limit exceeds the Last Price then the stock is already too high. Our objective is to buy low and the buy limit keeps us on the low end."

Company	Stock Symbol	52WK High	52WK Low	Last Price	Buy Limit	Buy Rank
Walmart	WMT	58.75	41.50	55.00	45.81	-21.30
Kmart	KM	13.55	4.75	6.08	6.95	3.95
Target	TGT	40.43	26.00	38.15	29.61	-23.68
Intel	INTC	47.87	18.96	31.76	26.18	-7.71
Adv Micro	AMD	34.65	7.69	13.21	14.43	1.81
Micron Tech	MU	49.61	16.39	26.73	24.70	-2.45
Best Buy	BBY	71.60	21.00	69.90	33.65	-28.66
Radio Shack	RSH	56.50	20.10	28.69	29.20	0.56
Circuit City	CC	20.25	8.69	16.58	11.58	-17.30
Barns & Nobl	BKS	43.99	21.63	27.01	27.22	0.38
Borders	BGP	24.43	10.87	18.60	14.26	-12.79
Amazon	AMZN	30.75	5.51	11.59	11.82	0.36
Sun Micro	SUNW	48.13	7.52	13.16	17.67	4.44
Dell	DELL	31.32	16.01	25.99	19.84	-16.07
IBM	IBM	119.90	80.06	112.15	90.02	-22.22

Wayne's Prospect List

Sara was disappointed. "I see you have Intel on your list. Just how bad is a Buy Rank of -7.71?"

"Not acceptable. Notice that the Buy Limit is 26.18. That's the most we would pay for Intel at this time."

"Oh," Sara said with a slight frown. "That's too bad. You know we have 500 shares of Intel I inherited from Aunt Candace. Wonder how much we could make selling calls on those 500 shares?"

"That's right," Wayne replied. "I had forgotten about that stock. Even though we wouldn't buy it at the current price we can consider selling calls. I'll do the computations while you fix us a cup of coffee."

A few minutes later Sara was back with coffee, cheese and crackers as Wayne put the final touches on his analysis.

"Intel closed today at $31.76. I decided to use that as our purchase price in the formula although since we inherited the stock we don't really have any investment cost in it. For tax purposes if we were to sell we would have the cost basis used in the estate tax return but I don't know what that is right now"

Sara looked at the table and immediately said, "Wow, look at Apr 30. Wayne how much is 500 times $4.70?

"$2,350", Wayne replied.. "That's new money. Money we don't have now. But I'm not sure that's the best choice. This is very confusing. How do we know which of the six choices is best? I wonder what the professor would do."

Intel Corp INTC Date: 11-28-01			
Month/Strike	Bid	%If Sold	% If Expired
Dec 30	2.60	.026	.081
Dec 32.50	1.15	.059	.036
Jan 30	3.40	.051	.107
Jan 32.50	2.00	.086	.062
Apr 30	4.70	.092	.147
Apr 32.50	3.40	.130	.107

Wayne took a bite of a cheese and cracker and puzzled over the table. He was concentrating so hard on the Intel analysis he didn't hear Sara leave to answer the phone. She soon came bustling back with a big grin.

"Wayne you are not going to believe who was on the phone. Rob and Jean Graham have just invited us over to their condo for lunch tomorrow. They have someone they want us to meet."

7

"Create your own vision of happiness."

Jean Groenke

Riding up the glass elevator to the Graham's penthouse condo, Sara and Wayne had a panoramic view of Marco Island. On their left was the Yacht Club at the foot of the Jolley Bridge, which connected the island to the mainland of southwest Florida. They saw a small jet which had taken off from the Naples Airport, about 20 miles to the north. The owner apparently wanted a view of Marco before making a sharp turn to the north. On their right they could see all the way to Goodland, a small community also on the island with another bridge connecting to the mainland. The elevator was for the exclusive use of the two penthouse condos at the top of the most recent luxury tower built on the beach. As they stepped out onto the open foyer they had views of the beautiful crescent beach to the north and the south.

"I wonder who they want us to meet", said Sara as Wayne pushed the door bell. Before the melodic chime had ended Jean Graham opened the door and warmly welcomed them in.

"Come in," she smiled. "We are so glad you could come over. I've heard about you, Wayne, from my husband. And Sara, what a beautiful sundress. Did you get it here on the island? Wayne, Rob is on the balcony. Why don't you go on out. There's a glass of ice tea waiting for you out there. We'll join you in a moment." Jean had the graceful

53

movements of a ballerina as she motioned Wayne in the direction of the balcony.

Wayne left the two women to get acquainted as he walked across the wide expanse of the Great Room. The view outside was magnificent but he was mainly intrigued by the wide collection of paintings and artifacts. He quickly noticed items from the Orient, Australia and Europe. *World travelers*, he decided.

As he stepped out onto the balcony he had the commanding view of the gulf to the west. The noon sun was just high enough to begin casting its rays on the west balcony. Rob called from the corner to the north. "Come around here Wayne. We can have the shade and still enjoy the view."

As Wayne took a comfortable seat, Rob set his book aside and said, "We've always been so rushed in our prior meetings. Maybe this afternoon we can have a good visit. I've wanted to ask you about your book. You mentioned that you sold your CPA firm and moved to Marco to write a novel."

Mention of the CPA firm brought back many mixed emotions for Wayne. There was the satisfaction of serving his clients and the frustration of having to jump through so many senseless – and sometimes contradictory – hoops. *Like a trained show dog,* he thought.

"Yes, well, I seem to have writer's block here lately. The novel idea comes from my work experience. After graduation from University of Minnesota, I worked for a small accounting firm while preparing to pass the test to be a Certified Public Accountant. The company I was working for had experienced accountants who specialized in auditing, small business "write-up" work and management advisory services. It just so happened that they were weak in the area of tax planning. That was the void that I filled. I was soon the tax specialist. When I started my own firm I continued on in the tax field.

"Just about every year there would be major changes in the tax law. At CPE classes, that's continuing professional education classes, these new tax laws were jokingly referred to as 'The Accountants and Tax Lawyers Relief Act'. That always rankled me. The thought that I was somehow receiving a government subsidy. And then I had to agree that I was indeed receiving a subsidy. The whole tax industry, from the simplest tax preparer to the most elaborate scheme for corporate, estate or personal tax avoidance, is a clear example of what's become known as corporate welfare."

Looking down at the gulf Wayne could see a pelican diving for a fish. *Now that's an honest living*, he thought. *No bureaucracies and no taxes. The pelican keeps what it earns and earns what it keeps.*

"So my novel is based in the world of public accountants and hopefully exposes what I see as serious flaws in the tax system."

"That's interesting," Rob commented. "But it's liable to get you the nick name of 'Don Quixote'. So many different groups have such a vested interest in a complicated tax system that I doubt it could ever be changed." Rob stood up and looked out at the gulf and down the beach.

"Wayne, bring the binoculars over. They are right there by your chair. Looks like a sail boat race is about to begin."

Wayne joined Rob at the railing and they took turns looking at the sailboats in fierce competition about half way to the horizon. Looking down the beach they could see sun bathers of all descriptions and swimmers enjoying the surf. Just below them a volley ball game was in progress with six girls playing against six local guys. The girl's team was in training for the summer Olympics and would no doubt handily defeat the local champions.

"You know Wayne," Rob said, handing him the binoculars, "when there is so much beauty in the world it's hard to get caught up in crusades to make changes. If there is a drawback to living on Marco maybe that's it. It's so easy to go with the flow and enjoy life. I enjoy focusing on my investments and spending time with Jean. We keep up with the kids and grandkids. What more does a man need in life? Maybe that's why you have writer's block on your novel. Lighten up. Enjoy life."

Jean and Sara joined them with a platter of sandwiches and pitcher of iced tea. "My specialty," said Jean. "Turkey on wheat with provolone cheese, lettuce, tomatoes and mayonnaise. I hope you like them."

Rob embraced Sara with a friendly hug. "So you are the reason my former student here received a B instead of an A in Finance 101. Well Wayne I can certainly understand your predicament." They all laughed, enjoying the conversation along with the food.

As the sandwiches were finished up Sara was the first to broach the subject of options. "Rob, we've been learning about your investment strategy. Last night when you called Wayne was explaining to me his understanding of the strategy and we were stumped by a particular problem. Do you mind if we ask you a question?'

"Sure. I thought you might have some questions. I will be glad to share what I've learned about the options market. I don't offer any guarantees but it has sure worked for us."

Wayne pulled the sheet of paper out of his pocket on which he had computed the various strike prices and dates for the 500 shares of Intel he and Sara owned. He unfolded the paper and handed it to the professor.

Intel Corp INTC		Date: 11-28-01	
Month/Strike	Bid	%If Sold	% If Expired
Dec 30	2.60	.026	.081
Dec 32.50	1.15	.059	.036
Jan 30	3.40	.051	.107
Jan 32.50	2.00	.086	.062
Apr 30	4.70	.092	.147
Apr 32.50	3.40	.130	.107

"Professor, we have 500 shares of Intel which we inherited several years back. I did the computations using the current price of $31.76 as the purchase price in the formulas. We are ready to sell calls on this stock. But how do we figure which of these six possibilities to select?"

Rob smiled. "You need my Magic Chart. Just a moment I'll get you a copy." Rob walked into his office and returned a moment later.

"What is a good premium for a covered call? That question plagued me for the first couple of years I was selling options. This area is mostly science and a little art. Our goal in selling calls is to generate a number of small gains on a continuous basis. If you want a larger premium the time factor will be longer. *Time IS Money*. How do we strike a balance between time and the overall gain? Through experience on simulating multiple option cycles and allowing for losses I have developed the following rate of return rate table for option premiums. This table is structured by current month and allows you to quickly determine if the rate of return on the option being considered is acceptable. It does not consider risk, so picking the right stock is also key. For improving our odds of picking the right stock we use the Buy Limit and Buy Rank computations. This table has successfully generated an average gain of 25% or more per year over a seven-year period."

Rob handed Wayne an index size card with a chart on the front and the back. One side was for the months January through June. The other side had the months July through December.

Wayne found the November column on side two. He went down the column to December and then across to the required percentages. One month out required a return of .068 if sold and .054 if expired. The closest he came was the December 32.50 premium of $1.15 which yielded .059 and .036 respectively. He checked for January by again going to the November column and reading down to January, then across to the required percentages. The chart required .084 and .067. The January 32.50 came very close with returns of .086 and .062. Good enough if sold and almost good enough if expired. He noticed that the April 32.50 premium of $3.40 was also very close.

"Professor, it looks like our best bet is January 32.50 but that doesn't quite meet the standard set by the Magic Chart."

THE MAGIC CHART – SIDE ONE

MONTHS TO EXP.	IF SOLD	IF EXP.	JAN	FEB	MAR	APR	MAY	JUN
1	.068	.054	FEB	MAR	APR	MAY	JUN	JUL
2	.084	.067	MAR	APR	MAY	JUN	JUL	AUG
3	.100	.080	APR	MAY	JUN	JUL	AUG	SEP
4	.116	.093	MAY	JUN	JUL	AUG	SEP	OCT
5	.134	.107	JUN	JUL	AUG	SEP	OCT	NOV
6	.150	.120	JUL	AUG	SEP	OCT	NOV	DEC
7	.166	.133	AUG	SEP	OCT	NOV	DEC	JAN
8	.184	.147	SEP	OCT	NOV	DEC	JAN	FEB
9	.200	.160	OCT	NOV	DEC	JAN	FEB	MAR

THE MAGIC CHART – SIDE TWO

MONTHS TO EXP.	IF SOLD	IF EXP.	JUL	AUG	SEP	OCT	NOV	DEC
1	.068	.054	AUG	SEP	OCT	NOV	DEC	JAN
2	.084	.067	SEP	OCT	NOV	DEC	JAN	FEB
3	.100	.080	OCT	NOV	DEC	JAN	FEB	MAR
4	.116	.093	NOV	DEC	JAN	FEB	MAR	APR
5	.134	.107	DEC	JAN	FEB	MAR	APR	MAY
6	.150	.120	JAN	FEB	MAR	APR	MAY	JUN
7	.166	.133	FEB	MAR	APR	MAY	JUN	JUL
8	.184	.147	MAR	APR	MAY	JUN	JUL	AUG
9	.200	.160	APR	MAY	JUN	JUL	AUG	SEP

"I'm not too surprised," Rob replied. "You see you made your computations on November 28. November calls expired on November 16. Remember "Time is Money". Since the November 16th expiration date you had already lost almost two weeks of time value. That is to say the premiums you found from your computations had already eroded in value because of the passage of two weeks. So the time remaining to the next expiration date is less than a full month. That means your return is actually a little greater that what you computed. So I would say if you take action right away you are justified in going with the January 32.50 contract. You'll pick a cool thousand dollars off the money tree. If the price of Intel remains at or below $32.50 through January 18, 2002, you can then sell April or July calls and pick some more money off the Intel money tree."

"What if our 500 shares of Intel get called," asked Sara. "What if it goes up to $40 a share and someone else gets the benefit of all that appreciation?"

"That may well happen," Rob responded. "In fact you can certainly expect it to happen on at least some of your calls. But there is no way of knowing in advance which stocks will go up sharply. My strategy, as I mentioned earlier, is **to generate a number of small gains on a continuous basis.**

"Look again at Wayne's computations for the percentage gain on the Jan 32.50 contract. Now ask yourself a basic question. Do you want to hold the stock without selling a call option on the chance that it may go up above $32.50, knowing that it could just as likely go down as up? Or do you want to lock in a gain of at least 6.2% for a period of, let's see, about 50 days? That's better than you could get on a CD for a whole year.

"To specifically answer your question about what to do if your stock gets called, that's the purpose of having a prospect list. Your cash position is greater by, first, the $1000 you receive from selling the calls and, second, by the sell of 500 shares for $32.50 a share. That's a total of $17,250. A stock that has risen sharply may now be above the Buy Limit and not have a satisfactory Buy Rank. If so you would use the money to buy a different stock with a good Buy Rank. Now you have the compounding effect of selling calls on stock purchased with the $1000 premium as well as the principle.

"Since it looks like you may be about to make your first foray into the options market, we had better talk about some of the technical terms you will encounter."

"Wait a minute," Jean interjected. "How about a slice of key lime pie for dessert. And I think it's getting a little warm here. Why don't we move inside and be more comfortable."

As they moved inside Sara commented to Wayne, "Maybe we can plant our own money tree, starting with those 500 shares of Intel?"

8

"That some should be rich shows that others may become rich, and hence is just encouragement to industry and enterprise." A. Lincoln

As the two couples settled down on luxurious leather couches, Rob proceeded to explain the technical aspects of options trading.

"Options are traded in the financial world the same as stocks at the Chicago Board Options Exchange (CBOE), American Stock Exchange (AMEX), Philadelphia and Pacific exchanges. Option orders are placed in your brokerage account and executed on an appropriate exchange. Not all stocks have options, so one needs to check availability by asking a stockbroker or accessing a quote service over the Internet such as at www.wallstreetcity.com or www.cboe.com.

"Buying and selling options is a little different from buying and selling stock. You usually just buy and sell stocks at a desired price. Option orders however require additional specifications such as expiration month, strike price, and intent (open or closing transaction). This information is communicated through the option symbol and specification of the order being placed.

"Stock and Index option symbols are composed of several different components representing the underlying security and information about the specific option contract. The first two or three letters of an option symbol are the option root, followed by the expiration month code, followed by the strike price code. Strike prices can vary depending on such factors as stock splits and sharp price moves etc. NYSE stocks use their stock symbol as their option root. For example Johnson & Johnson is JNJ, AT&T is T, Boeing is BA, and Wal-Mart is WMT. NASDAQ stocks use three letter option roots assigned by the exchange. For example the option root for Applied Materials is ANQ and for Microsoft is MSQ.

"So an Option Symbol is composed of the Option Root, followed by month code, followed by strike price code."

Rob paused, noticing the confused looks from Wayne and Sara. Jean broke the awkward silence with a suggestion. "Rob, dear, why don't you use the Illustrator I gave you for your birthday?"

"Good suggestion. Maybe this will help, Wayne and Sara." With that he picked up what looked like leather bound book. Opening it he pushed a button and a large painting on the wall nearest them, a beautiful impressionist painting of a family skiing in the Swiss Alps, turned into a clear three foot by five foot screen.. As Rob wrote in the Illustrator the information appeared on the screen for all to see.

"Here's the basic notation for expiration month codes," Rob said as he accessed a database. For each month there is one letter of the alphabet to signify a Call and a different letter to signify a Put.

	CALLS	PUTS
January	A	M
February	B	N
March	C	O
April	D	P
May	E	Q
June	F	R
July	G	S
August	H	T
September	I	U
October	J	V
November	K	W
December	L	X

"Then we use the letters again for stock price codes. One letter of the alphabet represents three possible prices. You will quickly get the hang of it."

A	5, 105, 205	N	70, 170, 270
B	10, 110, 210	O	75, 175, 275
C	15, 115, 215	P	80, 180, 280
D	20, 120, 220	Q	85, 185, 285
E	25, 125, 225	R	90, 190, 290
F	30, 130, 230	S	95, 195, 295
G	35, 135, 235	T	100, 200, 300
H	40, 140, 240	U	7.50, 37.50, 67.50
I	45, 145, 245	V	12.50, 42.50, 72.50
J	50, 150, 250	W	17.50, 47.50, 77.50
K	55, 155, 255	X	22.50, 52.50, 82.50
L	60, 160, 260	Y	27.50, 57.50, 87.50
M	65, 165, 265	Z	32.50, 62.50, 92.50

"Notice how this works in the following examples. In the first one, WMTLJ, the WMT stands for Wal-Mart, the "L" stands for December Call, and the J indicates a price of 50, 150 or 250, whichever one makes sense relative to the price of Wal-Mart stock. Of course that's 50.

66

WMTLJ	Wal-Mart December 50 Call
WMTXI	Wal-Mart December 45 Put

MSQIN	Microsoft September 70 Call
MSQXL	Microsoft December 60 Put

THD	AT&T August 20 Call
TVW	AT&T October 17.50 Put

"Options quotes can be found in the newspaper or on the Internet at www.cboe.com or www.wallstreetcity.com."

Wayne raised his hand to ask a question and then with an embarrassed grin brought it back down. "Professor, that word "Put" has got me confused. I believe I am beginning to understand Calls. But what is a Put?"

"My personal options strategy," Rob replied, "involves both Calls and Puts. I haven't talked to you about Puts because I believe for the first year you are in the options market you should only do Calls, and only covered calls at that. So for now let me just say that there are two types of stock options, Puts and Calls. A Call is an option to *buy* a stock at a given price for a certain period of time. A Put is an option to *sell* a stock at a given price for a certain period of time."

Rob pushed a few buttons and the following matrix appeared on the screen:

67

CALLS		
Buy a Call You have the right to purchase a stock at a specified price for a certain period of time.	**Write (sell) a Call** You have an obligation to sell a stock at a specified price for a certain period of time, if the buyer activates the Call.	
Buy a Put You have the right to sell a stock at a specified price for a certain period of time.	**Write (sell) a Put** You have a obligation to buy a stock at a specified price for a certain period of time, if the buyer activates the Put	
PUTS		

(Left margin: BUY — Right margin: SELL)

"The strategy that I am recommending to you is called a covered call. That means that on stock that you own you are selling a Call, that is you are selling someone else the right to buy your stock. That's the top right quadrant of the matrix. I have developed strategies that involve all quadrants. But I strongly suggest that you get the basics down for doing covered calls and then we can talk about other strategies."

Wayne nodded agreement and Rob continued. "Now before you run off to place your trade, it might be good to understand how option orders should be placed."

"When placing option trading orders it is very important to state exactly what is intended. If a mistake is made and you execute a wrong trade you may incur a loss to undo it.

"Option orders like stock orders can be placed in your brokerage account over the phone by calling a trader, over the phone with direct keypad input, or over the Internet with on line access to your account. No matter which way you trade the way an order is placed is important. I'll put on the screen some basic definitions."

As Rob pushed points in the notebook the following items appeared on the screen.

Sell to Open – You are opening a short position for a specific option. For example this is what you use to write a covered call.

Buy to Close – You are buying back an option you previously sold, to close out the option. For example this is what you would do if you did not want your stock to be called. Also, you would want to do this if you want to sell the stock. Selling the stock without buying back the call option would leave you in a high risk uncovered position.

Buy to Open – You are opening a long position for a specific option. For example this is what you do when you are taking a leveraged position by buying the option instead of the stock.

Sell to Close – You are closing a long position for a specific option. For example this is what you do to capture a gain on your leveraged position.

Market order – The order will be executed at the next available bid price. Use this to buy or sell immediately.

Limit order – The order is executed at the limit price or better if possible.

For the day – The order will expire at the end of the trading day.

All or none (AON) – Buy or sell the number of contracts specified. This condition is used to reduce the possibility of trading only one or a small number of contracts in a multiple contract order. Additional orders may increase your overall commission cost.

Good till canceled (GTC) – The order is open until it is canceled. Most brokerage firms will close GTC orders after ninety days.

"Considering what we've learned so far, your order to sell calls on your 500 shares of Intel stock might be as follows:

"Sell to open, 5 Intel January 32.50 Calls (INQAZ) at a limit of $2.00, for the day, all or none.

"INQ is the symbol assigned to Intel options. "A" indicates that it is a January Call. "Z" gives us the price of $32.50

"This order would be filled when someone wants to buy 5 Intel January 32.50 Calls for $2.00 or more. If the market has moved down when the order is placed it may not fill. If the market is moving up it could fill at $2.00 or even higher. If it is not filled before the end of the day it expires.

"A future order to close out this position could be as follows:

"Buy to close, 5 Intel January 32.50 Calls (INQAZ) at the market for the day.

"This order would be filled at the next available ask price for the option. Since it is a market order the actual price for each of the 5 contracts may be different. Also it may be only partial filled."

"Professor, why would we want to buy to close an option?" asked Wayne.

"This is an example of managing your accounts while you are waiting for the expiration date. A wise old investor was once asked what he thought the stock market would do. His response was: 'It will fluctuate.' And indeed it will. The stock on which you have sold a covered call will fluctuate in value. As the stock fluctuates so does the premium, or price of the call option. For example you expect to receive $2.00 a share for your call options on Intel. In a few days or weeks that same option, INQAZ, may be trading for 50 cents or less. If you think the stock is going to come roaring back, bringing the value of the option with it, then "buy to close" at the lower price and sell again later at the higher premium.

"Okay, let's move on to some record keeping checklists I recommend. A disciplined approach is desirable in preparing an option order to prevent mistakes. Here are the steps I go through in preparing a trade:

1. Write down the trade that you intend to execute.

2. Get a quote on the stock and intended option. This will validate the option symbol, strike price, and strike month.

3. Calculate the return on each premium.

4. Determine if a market or limit order is appropriate.

5. Set the price on your order and then submit it.

"For example, you have 500 shares of Intel in your account. You want to place a January covered call option trade and you do not want to have your stock called for less than $30.00 per share. Now you write down the option quotes you need to make a decision.

Intel stock symbol is – INTC

Intel January $30 call symbol is – INQAF

Intel January $32.50 call symbol is – INQAZ

Intel January $35 call symbol is – INQAG

"You go to your quote provider (by phone or over the Internet) request the quote for each symbol and write it down."

Rob punched some numbers on the notepad. "Here is an earlier computation I had made on Intel."

INTC   28.80 – 28.83 Last trade 28.80 up .03

INTC JAN 30 Call   INQAF 3.50 - 3.60

INTC JAN 32.50 Call   INQAZ 2.50 - 2.65

INTC JAN 35 Call   INQAG 1.75 - 1.90

"I've created a program I call the Call Option Wizard which computes gain, if called and if expired, for any combination of strike price and expiration date. It also compares the resulting percentages to my Magic Chart. Just to refresh your memory here is the formula we use to compute the gains."

If Sold =	$\dfrac{(\text{Strike Price} + \text{Premium} - \text{Purchase Price})}{\text{Purchase Price}}$
If Expired =	$\dfrac{\text{Premium}}{\text{Purchase Price}}$.

"Here are the results based on a purchase price of $28.83."

Option	Call Option Premium	Called Gain	Expired Gain
JAN 30	$3.50	16.1%	12.10%
JAN 32.50	$2.50	21.4%	8.67%
JAN 35	$1.75	27.4%	6.07%

"You look at the Magic Chart table and determine which call option best fits *the money tree* model.

"Since Intel is currently in an up trend you decide that a limit order at 3.50 should be filled within seconds.

"You write your order as follows:

"Sell 5 INTC January 30 Calls to open at $3.50 for the day all or none.

"Now place your order and write its confirmation number on your order sheet.

73

"When your order is filled write out the detail of the order and the net proceeds of the action on your daily-completed order sheet. Save these sheets until you receive your confirmation from your broker. This is a precautionary measure only. If there are errors in the confirmation you need documentation to perform resolution. You will also need your daily trade results sheet to update your trading files and track your overall results.

"After I started trading options it became important to record and track each and every trade. I have done this since day one and now have the history of every trade I made in my blue file. Why a blue file? For every trade you execute you will receive a trade confirmation in the mail from your broker. To keep these together and easily accessible I put them in a blue file folder instead of the standard cream colored ones. This allowed me to find this file very quickly since I was using it more and more each day. I also have a box on the daily order sheets, which gets checked indicating that the blue file was updated.

"In this blue file folder I have a transaction history tracking sheet on which I record my daily transactions such as, stock buys, call option sales, assignments, close outs, etc. I record the date, the transaction, and the net debit or credit for the trade. This is a running list and fills multiple pages for the year. After receiving the confirmation from the broker I use a highlighter and highlight the debit or credit on the tracking sheet to indicate that I received the trade confirmation and the results agree. The confirmations are filed in the order of the tracking sheet. This allows quick access if a reference is required. If a transaction is not highlighted within two weeks, I call the brokerage house and ask for a duplicate confirmation. It may not have been sent or it may have gotten lost in the mail. This process makes sure there is a paper trail for every transaction for tax or other purposes such as stockholder class action lawsuits. In the latter situation, you may be asked to provide copies of all transactions during a certain period to substantiate a possible claim and participate in any settlement. My greatest use of this record was the settlement on litigation regarding the NASDAQ market makers spread price fixing antitrust action. This is where the US Department of Justice brought a civil enforcement proceeding on July 17, 1996, alleging that twenty-four NASDAQ market makers, together with others, conspired to widen spreads in violation of the federal antitrust laws. To participate in this settlement, one had to supply detail records of related NASDAQ stock transactions for the defined period.

"The blue file contains all transactions in the order of execution by date. I also maintain a group of computer files called directory nineteen. In this directory I maintain a file by company of every transaction executed. From this directory I can extract every trade on any company that I have invested in and print out the trading history and corresponding overall gain or loss. I process this directory on a periodic basis to update my successful company list and to track overall results. I use the stock symbol as the file name, which prevents duplication while still being very informative. I backup this directory monthly and keep multiple backups for history and recovery if needed. All of the examples I've shown you are from this history file."

There was a buzz from someone downstairs wanting to come up. Jean excused herself.

Rob continued. "One other important record keeping requirement is a tax file. For taxes you need to actually move some cash from your brokerage account to a savings or money market account. This way you are not tempted to invest it. It is reserved for taxes so leave it there. You do not want to have to close out some calls and sell some stock in April to pay the taxes. It could be bad timing. Remember we are reserving for taxes because we plan to make money. It is one of the perks when you have gains. The amount to reserve depends on your tax bracket but here is good formula:

"Tax Reserve = (Total Option Premiums –Losses) x 25%"

"Speaking of taxes," Jean said jokingly as she returned with the visitor.

Except for the long hair worn in a ponytail and the diamond stud in his left ear, the man looked like Rob Graham.

Rob rose with a smile and said, "Wayne, Sara, I would like to introduce by twin brother, Greg. Greg these are our friends, Wayne and Sara Kimball."

As hands were being shook Rob continued. "Greg is a distinguished professor of mathematics. He has been working on a formula that I think you will be interested in."

9

Mens sana in corpore sano – a sound mind in a
sound body - *is the greatest wealth on earth.*   Wade Keller

"Look at these incredible shells I found on Sand
Dollar Island. And the birds. I can't get over it. You people
actually live here. I'm just now beginning to relax. Soon I'll
be back in the frozen north land."

Greg's New England pale skin had taken on a Marco
Island tan in the week he had been visiting. Jean brought
coffee for everyone and a slice of pie for Greg.

As the group settled back down Rob picked up his
leather note pad. "Greg has developed a formula that I
believe will be very valuable.

"Wayne you know how important it is to pick the
right stock. That's where I put my greatest emphasis. First
build a qualified prospect list. Then qualify the list with Buy
Limit and Buy Rank formulas. And finally you want to be
sure the current price has crossed over the fifty day moving
average."

"I'm with you up to this point," said Wayne. "I've
done all the homework although I haven't put it into practice
yet."

Rob continued. "There are a lot of times when
looking at a stock chart with a fifty-day moving average that
I notice that the current price is below the Buy Limit and the
fifty-day average. The stock is a prime prospect but the time
for action is not quite here. How can I tell when it is time to

act? I do not want to be too late but not too early either. I always felt there should be some way to combine the value of the Buy Rank with the fifty day moving average.

"I was inspired one evening when Jean and I were out walking and saw a shooting star, a small meteorite flashing across the earth's atmosphere. Some meteorites are reflected with a flash and others enter the atmosphere and display a burning tail as they near the earth. Why not develop a Take Action Indicator that signals when you should proceed with buying a stock and selling a covered call based on the current price approaching the buy limit and fifty-day moving average. As the price nears these values action should be taken. The challenge was putting the information into a formula that would give a reliable and consistent ranking.

"So when Greg came for a visit I knew he would soon be bored without a math challenge."

Greg smiled and sipped his coffee.

"Greg, why don't you explain it from here," said Rob as he handed over the note pad.

"I should explain that, thanks to brother Rob, I have been supplementing my teaching income for the past year with options trading. In the back of my mind was the thought that there should be something more definitive than the Buy Rank for taking action. But I hadn't actually made the conceptual leap until Rob explained the objective.

"There is an ideal situation and then next best. The ideal situation is when the buy rank is greater than five, the fifty-day average is flat or increasing, and the current price has just crossed it.

"The next best is when the buy rank is positive and the current price is nearing or has just moved above the 50 day moving average. So here's the formula." Greg punched a few buttons on the note pad and the following formula appeared on the screen.

$$TAI = \frac{(CP)(CP) + 3(FDA)(BL - CP) - (BL)(CP)}{(CP)(L-BL) + 2(FDA)(BL - L)}$$

Greg continued as if it were the simplest thing in the world. "TAI stands for Take Action Indicator. CP is the current price of the stock that you are considering. FDA is the fifty-day moving average. BL is the Buy Limit and L is the fifty two week low."

With a look of utter despair Wayne said, "Greg please. By the time I figure out this formula we'll be at the next expiration date."

"Oh", replied Greg in mock surprise. "Did you want the simple version? Well as a matter of fact I did get it a little simpler. In this one BR stands for Buy Rank."

$$TAI = BR \left(1 + \frac{FDA}{2(FDA) - CP} \right)$$

"Thanks Greg," said Rob. "I've tried it out and so far it works great. Remember when looking at the buy rank by itself, I said anytime it was positive it was good and above five it was great. The take action indicator is a little different.

79

We want to take action when it is between 10 and −5, be cautious (wait) when it is between −5 and −10, and look at other opportunities if it is less than −10. If the TAI has a value above 10 it may still be okay to precede with this prospect but a second review of the fifty-two week price chart with the fifty-day moving average is in order to see if the stock is still in a downward trend. We may be too early so we want to verify it before we act.

"Here's what you are looking for on the TAI."

Rob wrote in his note pad and the following appeared on the screen.

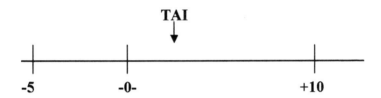

"Actually I can make it even easier for you. I have developed a software program that takes all the work out of computing Buy Limit, Buy Rank and TAI. I call it the Prospect List Manager. For each stock in your portfolio and prospect list you simply plug in the fifty two week low, fifty two week high and the fifty day moving average. The program computes Buy Limit, Buy Rank and TAI. You can sort the prospect list by any column. That makes it easy to decide which stock to add to your portfolio and which stocks in your portfolio you should sell."

Rob closed his note pad Illustrator and the screen became a live scene of a cabin on a lake in Minnesota. Ice cycles hung from the eves of the cabin and a cold rain was blowing across the frozen lake. Looking at Greg he said, "Does it make you homesick, brother?"

10

"You cannot predict the future, but you can plan the events that shape it."   Ron Groenke

The setting sun on the clear waters of the Caribbean was matched by the rising of a glorious full moon. Wayne and Sara enjoyed the view as they walked across the top deck of the cruise ship where they were to meet Rob and Jean. Over the past year they had repeatedly sold calls on the 500 shares of Intel stock, their first venture in the options market. With the Professor's assistance they had developed a portfolio of over thirty stocks which met their investment criteria and had a good yield in call premiums. Part of the monthly premium income was used for living expenses and the remainder was reinvested.

"Hurry, come look at the dolphins," Jean called to Wayne and Sara from the port side of the deck. The dolphins seemed to be enjoying racing along with the fairly small luxury cruise ship. There were only 400 passengers and an equal number of staff and crew. The whole purpose of the cruise was the investment seminars sponsored by one of the major investment publications. Wayne had written an article for the national magazine titled "The Professor's Money Tree" which resulted in Rob being invited to be one of the lecturers on the cruise.

"These are really posh accommodations," exclaimed Sara. "Now if I could just get these nautical terms right. Like how do you know which side is port and which side is starboard?"

The two couples enjoyed the beauty of the sky and the frolicking of the dolphins. Their destination was Grand Cayman. But the real purpose of the trip was to provide a pleasant setting for the financial seminars.

"I heard a bit of trivia once that helps me with those terms, port and starboard," said Rob. "And it has to do with the word 'posh' that you just used Sara. "When cruise ships first started going out of London down the coast of Europe and through the straits of Gibraltar, the first class passengers wanted to be on the side of the ship with a view of the coast. Naturally they would be on the port or left side going down. Then on the return cruise home they would change to the staterooms on the right or starboard side of the ship so they would still have a view of the coast. The term 'port out starboard home' or simply posh, became synonymous with first class accommodations."

One of the staff came by with a tray of drinks and hors d'oeuvres. As they walked along the deck Wayne commented to Rob, "You really got a lot of response last night on your lecture 'Make Your Own Dividends'. I could tell that was a real eye opener for most of the audience. What will you talk about in tonight's lecture?"

"You remember there was an important question asked the first night in the opening session that is typically not covered in these seminars. In fact the guy made the point that he had read a lot of books about making money in the stock market. All the systems he had read about never took into account that the market goes down as well as up, that you can and do have real losses in the stock market. I have developed a software program that simulates stock investments and the subsequent sell of covered calls. You can alter the various factors, including a stock loss, and see the resulting portfolio gain or loss over a period of time. My Illustrator works with the ships video system so I can run the simulation based on questions from the audience in real time."

"What about the Cedric Chart? Are you going to show that?" Wayne had been amazed at the apparent accuracy of the Buy/Sell time line chart of unknown origin, perhaps made as early as the Civil War.

"Hmmm. The five fat years. It might be interesting to get the reaction of this sophisticated group of investors."

Their conversation was interrupted by the familiar ship's bell that indicated the captain was about to make an announcement.

"This is the Captain speaking. Tonight's lecture by Dr. Robert Graham has been moved to the Main Theater to facilitate the increased demand. Dr. Charles Jackson's lecture on "Selecting the Right Mutual Fund" will now be held in Stateroom B."

****

Three seats had been reserved on the front row for Wayne, Sara and Jean. Rob walked immediately onto the stage and was introduced by the MC, Louis Ruckhammer.

"Ladies and Gentlemen. Professor Graham will speak tonight on the subject 'Simulate Your Trading Plan'. As you know, last night's topic, 'Create Your Own Dividends', has been the main topic of conversation all day. I'm sure that accounts for the overflow crowd tonight."

A murmur went through the audience. "Yes, yes", the moderator continued. "I know some of you found last night's topic to be a little controversial, especially those of you associated with old line full service brokerage houses." As most of the audience laughed, recalling the professor's blunt talk about the individual investor's ability to manage his own investment account, Louis winked at Rob. Rob smiled in return but otherwise maintained a professional decorum.

"Please welcome once again Professor Robert Graham."

The standing ovation surprised Rob. He quickly motioned for the audience to be seated so he could begin his presentation.

"Before I initiate a trade I simulate its effect on my portfolio for the next three years out. If I am selling a call on a stock I own, I want to know the effect of tying up the underlying value of the long stock position. If I write a six-month call option I know that the stock is committed and the plan is that it will be called. If it is called the cash received for the underlying stock value is used to buy a new position from my prospect list and again write covered calls. If the stock is not called I need to make a basic decision. I will either liquidate my position in the stock because of changes in the company and the marketplace or I sell a new call option. Selling a new call option requires a decision as to the new strike price and months to expiration. On some of my stocks I have sold covered calls over a dozen times. As one three month or six month call option expires I sell a new one. That generates a powerful compounding effect.

"All of these factors can be easily simulated in a program I have developed for just this purpose.

"Last night I talked to you about creating dividends on stocks that don't pay dividends. That's the money tree effect: generating income by selling covered calls. It's nice to have an orchard of money trees. Each month you can pluck some fruit from some of the trees in your orchard.

"But......" Rob paused to be sure he had everyone's full attention. "But suppose some of the trees go bad. By that I mean suppose some of the stocks you select in your portfolio go down in value. What effect will that have on our plan to generate a high rate of return on our investment? That's the purpose of the simulation. We want to gain confidence that we can generate a high return even if some of our stocks go bad.

"It is important to set down a goal. In most cases option values follow the normal ups and downs of the market, so let's be realistic in our expected gains. Is 20% possible? Yes. Is 30% possible? Yes. Is 50% possible? Yes, a 50% gain in one year on your investments with options is possible because I've been there, done that! Okay, what is realistic? Let's pick a goal of 25%. Would you agree that a 25% return on your stock portfolio would be pretty good?

"Here is the plan. We'll keep it simple for illustration purposes. We are going to take $25000 and buy three different stocks and sell covered calls. I like to have income coming in each month so for the first month I will sell a one month call on one stock, a two month call on the second stock and a three month call on the third stock. We'll assume we are starting in January. In February and subsequent months we will sell three month calls.

"We start the simulation with an initial investment of $25000."

Rob punched the number into his Illustrator and it flashed on the three large screens, one directly in front of the audience and two on each side. "We need to make a couple of assumptions. First how much premium as a percentage of the stock price could you expect to get for a three month option? My experience has been that you can fairly easily get 10% return for three months. You will need to test this yourself by checking the call premiums on some of your favorite stocks. You should easily get this information from your online broker. Or go to www.wallstreetcity.com You may find it easier to get, say, 4% for one month than 10% for three months. It all depends on stock volatility. The higher the volatility the greater the premium. Anyway for our simulation we will use 3.3% a month or 10% for three months.

"Now the next assumption is stock loss. Unless you are absolutely brilliant and extremely lucky, you will pick some stocks that insist on going down in value rather than up. I will use a 15% loss factor. That is the simulator will sell two of my stocks each year for a combined loss of 15% of the beginning of year portfolio value. Does that seem reasonable?"

There were murmurs of agreement through out the room.

"Now there is one other factor we need to consider. What about taxes? At the end of each year I will have the simulation deduct 25% of the net income – call premiums less stock losses - from the portfolio to keep the tax man happy. For simplicity I have ignored commission expense and gains from stock appreciation. Commissions are low if you use a good online broker and would be more than off set by gains from stock appreciation. Also in this particular simulation we are not using the leverage available in margin accounts."

As Rob finished punching numbers in the Illustrator the following was shown on the screen:

SIMULATION

PORTFOLIO GROWTH THROUGH
SELL OF COVERED CALLS

FACTORS:

1.   INITIAL INVESTMENT: $25,000

2.   10% PREMIUM PER QUARTER
(3.3% PER MONTH)

3.   ASSUMED STOCK LOSSES EACH YEAR
OF 15% OF BEGINNING BALANCE

4.   ASSUMED TAX OF 25% OF NET
INCOME (PREMIUMS LESS LOSSES)

"OK. Are you ready. Here comes the simulation for the first six months."

YEAR ONE

MONTH	TRANSACTION	AMT	BAL	INC
JAN	INITIAL INVESTMENT	25000	25000	
	BUY A & SELL MAR CALLS	-12500	12500	
	OPTIONS SOLD AT 6.7 %	837	13337	
	BUY B & SELL APR CALLS	-10670	2667	
	OPTIONS SOLD AT 10 %	1067	3734	
	BUY C & SELL FEB CALLS	- 3734	-0-	
	OPTIONS SOLD AT 3.3 %	123	123	
	OPTION PREM INCOME JAN			2027
FEB	STK C CALLED OR EXPIRED	3734	3857	
	STK C SELL MAY CALLS	- 3857	-0-	
	OPTIONS SOLD AT 10 %	385	385	
	OPTION PREM INCOME FEB			385
MAR	STK A CALLED OR EXPIRED	12500	12885	
	STK A SELL JUN CALLS	12885	-0-	
	OPTIONS SOLD AT 10 %	1288	1288	
	OPTION PREM INCOME MAR			1288
APR	STK B CALLED OR EXPIRED	10670	11958	
	STK B SELL JUL CALLS	11958	-0-	
	OPTIONS SOLD AT 10 %	1195	1195	
	OPTION PREM INCOME APR			1195
MAY	STK C CALLED OR EXPIRED	3857	5053	
	STK C SELL AUG CALLS	-5053	-0-	
	OPTIONS SOLD AT 10 %	505	505	
	OPTION PREM INCOME MAY			505
JUNE	STK A CALLED OR EXPIRED	12885	13391	
	STK A SELL SEP CALLS	-13391	-0-	
	OPTIONS SOLD AT 10 %	1339	1339	
	OPTION PREM INCOME JUN			1339

"Let's go over this first six months and I think you will quickly get the hang of it. In January we make an initial investment in our brokerage account of $25,000. We buy three stocks, A, B & C, carefully selected from our prospect list. You recall last night I talked briefly about my system of ranking stocks and use of the TAI formula. Stock selection is very important but for tonight's discussion we are focusing on the three year simulation.

"For our first purchase of stock A we sell March calls for a premium of 6.7%. For simplicity we are assuming the strike price is the same as the purchase price when in reality the strike price would frequently be about 5 to 10% above the purchase price.

"The premium received of $837 is added to our account balance and used in the purchase of stocks B & C. Thus the compounding effect begins the very first month. On stock B we sell April calls and on stock C we sell February calls. In subsequent months all calls will be for three months. By staggering the calls the first month and then selling three month options we are able to have premium income each month.

"Each stock will either be called, in which case we receive cash, or the option will expire. Either event leaves us in position to repeat the process, selling additional calls and reinvesting at least part of the premium received.

"Now let's take a look at the last six months and portfolio value at year end."

MONTH	TRANSACTION	AMT	BAL	INC
JULY	STK B CALLED OR EXPIRED	11958	13297	
	STK B SELL OCT CALLS	-13297	-0-	
	OPTIONS SOLD AT 10 %	1329	1329	
	OPTION PREM INCOME JUL			1329
AUG	STK C CALLED OR EXPIRED	5053	6383	
	STK C SELL NOV CALLS	-6383	-0-	
	OPTIONS SOLD AT 10 %	638	638	
	OPTION PREM INCOME AUG			638
SEP	STK A SOLD AT LOSS			
	(13391 - 1500)	11891	12529	
	NEW A SELL DEC CALLS	-10023	2505	
	OPTIONS SOLD AT 10 %	1002	3508	
	BUY D SELL DEC CALLS	-3508	-0-	
	OPTIONS SOLD AT 10 %	350	350	
	OPTION PREM INCOME SEP			1353
OCT	STK B SOLD AT LOSS			
	(13297 - 2250)	11047	11398	
	NEW B SELL JAN CALLS	-11398	-0-	
	OPTIONS SOLD AT 10 %	1139	1139	
	OPTION PREM INCOME OCT			1139
NOV	STK C CALLED OR EXPIRED	6383	7523	
	STK C SELL FEB CALLS	-7523	-0-	
	OPTIONS SOLD AT 10 %	752	752	
	OPTION PREM INCOME NOV			752
DEC	A&D CALLED OR EXPIRED	13531	14284	
	STK A&D SELL MAR CALLS	-14284	-0-	
	OPTIONS SOLD AT 10 %	1428	1428	
	TAX RESERVE	-2408	-980	
	OPTION PREM INCOME DEC			1428
TOTAL PREMIUM INCOME YEAR ONE				**13378**

PORTFOLIO VALUE AT YEAR END		
		BALANCE
STOCK A & D	14284	14284
STOCK B	11398	25682
STOCK C	7523	33205
CASH (DEC PREMIUMS)	1428	34633
25% TAX ON NET INCOME (PREMIUMS LESS LOSSES)	-2408	**32225**
ASSUMED STOCK LOSSES		3750
GAIN AFTER TAX & LOSS		7225
RETURN ON INVESTMENT		28.90%

"Notice the transactions in September and October. In those months we incur stock market losses of $1500 and $2250, 15% of the beginning of year portfolio balance. These losses reflect real life experiences. No matter how careful you are there will be stock market losses. For simulation purposes we have just assumed we will lose 15% each year. These losses could occur because the stock price went down and we decided to sell the stock. Perhaps the stock no longer meets our stock selection criteria such as profitable quarters or volume of trades. Another way we could have a loss is when the market price goes down and we decide to sell calls at a lower strike price than our original purchase price. If that happens and the stock is called we again have a stock loss. In that case the loss may well be offset by premium income, but it is still a loss. A stock market strategy is only worthwhile if it can overcome those losses and still show a significant gain.

"Notice in December we deduct $2,408 for tax reserve. This is 25% of net income, $13,378 premium income less the $3,750 stock losses. Taxes are even more certain than stock market losses. It's best to just accept the fact that you are going to make money and you will need to pay taxes. As the quantity of premium income increases you will probably need to make quarterly payments to the IRS. Plan ahead. Set aside a reserve for taxes so you aren't caught in a situation of having to liquidate some investments to pay taxes.

"Finally, how did we do for the year? Even after taxes and market losses our portfolio value has grown to $32,225, all from the sell of call options. We are ignoring the possibility of stock market appreciation.

"Our portfolio growth of $7,225 represents a return on investment of 28.9%. Let's move on to year two."

Rob flashed all of year two and the summary onto the screens

YEAR TWO

MONTH	TRANSACTION	AMT	BAL	INC
JAN	BALANCE FORWARD STK B CALLED OR EXPIRED STK B SELL APR CALLS OPTIONS SOLD AT 10 % OPTION PREM INCOME JAN	 11398 -10418 1041	-980 10418 -0- 1041	 1041
FEB	STK C CALLED OR EXPIRED STK C SELL MAY CALLS OPTIONS SOLD AT 10 % OPTION PREM INCOME FEB	7523 - 8565 856	8565 -0- 856	 856
MAR	A&D CALLED OR EXPIRED STK A SELL JUN CALLS OPTIONS SOLD AT 10 % STK D SELL JUN CALLS OPTIONS SOLD AT 10 % OPTION PREM INCOME MAR	14284 7570 757 8327 833	15140 7570 8327 -0- 833	 1590
APR	STK B SOLD AT A LOSS (10418 - 1450) STK B SELL JUL CALLS OPTIONS SOLD AT 10 % OPTION PREM INCOME APR	 8968 -9801 980	 9801 -0- 980	 980
MAY	STK C CALLED OR EXPIRED STK C SELL AUG CALLS OPTIONS SOLD AT 10 % OPTION PREM INCOME MAY	8565 -9545 954	9545 -0- 954	 954
JUNE	A & D CALLED OR EXPIRED STK A SELL SEP CALLS OPTIONS SOLD AT 10 % STK D SELL SEP CALLS OPTIONS SOLD AT 10 % OPTION PREM INCOME JUNE	15897 -8426 843 -9269 927	16852 8426 9269 -0- 927	 1770

MONTH	TRANSACTION	AMT	BAL	INC
JULY	STK B CALLED OR EXPIRED	9801	10728	
	STK B SELL OCT CALLS	–	-0-	
	OPTIONS SOLD AT 10 %	10728	1072	
	OPTION PREM INCOME JUL	1072		1072
AUG	STK C CALLED OR EXPIRED	9545	10617	
	STK C SELL NOV CALLS	–	-0-	
	OPTIONS SOLD AT 10 %	10617	1062	
	OPTION PREM INCOME AUG	1062		1062
SEP	A&D CALLED OR EXPIRED	17695	18757	
	NEW A SELL DEC CALLS	9378	9378	
	OPTIONS SOLD AT 10 %	938	10316	
	NEW D SELL DEC CALLS	10316	-0-	
	OPTIONS SOLD AT 10 %	1031	1031	
	OPTION PREM INCOME SEP			1969
OCT	STK B CALLED OR EXPIRED	10728	11759	
	STK B SELL JAN CALLS	11759	-0-	
	OPTIONS SOLD AT 10 %	1176	1176	
	OPTION PREM INCOME OCT			1176
NOV	STK C SOLD AT A LOSS			
	(10617 - 3384)	7234	8410	
	STK C SELL FEB CALLS	-8410	-0-	
	OPTIONS SOLD AT 10 %	841	841	
	OPTION PREM INCOME NOV			841
DEC	A&D CALLED OR EXPIRED	19694	20535	
	NEW A SELL MAR CALLS	10268	10267	
	OPTIONS SOLD AT 10 %	1027	11294	
	NEW D SELL MAR CALLS	11294	-0-	
	OPTIONS SOLD AT 10 %	1129	1129	
	TAX RESERVE	2659	-1530	
	OPTION PREM INCOME DEC			2156
TOTAL PREMIUM INCOME YEAR TWO				**15467**

94

PORTFOLIO VALUE AT YEAR END		
		BALANCE
STOCK A	10268	10268
STOCK B	11759	22027
STOCK C	8410	30437
STOCK D	11295	41732
CASH	1129	42861
25% TAX ON NET INCOME (PREMIUMS LESS LOSSES)	-2659	**40202**
ASSUMED STOCK LOSSES		4834
GAIN AFTER TAX & LOSS		7977
RETURN ON INVESTMENT		24.75%

"The key point here," Rob began, "is that the advantages of compounding are powerful but begin slowly. Our portfolio has grown by almost $8,000 or 24.75%. Accordingly we have larger stock losses and reserve for taxes.

"Let's go on to year three."

MONTH	TRANSACTION	AMT	BAL	INC
JAN	BALANCE FORWARD B CALLED OR EXPIRED STK B SELL APR CALLS OPTIONS SOLD AT 10 % OPTION PREM INCOME APR	 11759 -10229 1023 	-1530 10229 -0- 1023 	 1023
FEB	STK C CALLED OR EXPIRED STK C SELL MAY CALLS OPTIONS SOLD AT 10 % OPTION PREM INCOME FEB	8410 - 9433 943 	9433 -0- 943 	 943
MAR	A&D CALLED OR EXPIRED STK A SELL JUN CALLS OPTIONS SOLD AT 10 % STK D SELL JUN CALLS OPTIONS SOLD AT 10 % NEW E SELL JUN CALLS OPTIONS SOLD AT 10 % OPTION PREM INCOME MAR	21562 11253 1125 -9902 990 -3465 346 	22505 11252 12377 2475 3465 -0- 346 	 2462
APR	STK B CALLED OR EXPIRED STK B SELL JUL CALLS OPTIONS SOLD AT 10 % OPTION PREM INCOME APR	10230 -10576 1057 	10576 -0- 1057 	 1057
MAY	STK C CALLED OR EXPIRED STK C SELL AUG CALLS OPTIONS SOLD AT 10 % OPTION PREM INCOME MAY	9433 -10490 1049 	10490 -0- 1049 	 1049
JUNE	A&D CALLED OR EXPIRED STK A SELL SEP CALLS OPTIONS SOLD AT 10 % STK D SELL SEP CALLS OPTIONS SOLD AT 10 % STK E SELL SEP CALLS OPTIONS SOLD AT 10 % OPTION PREM INCOME JUN	24621 -12835 1283 -11295 1129 -3953 395 	25670 12835 14118 2824 3953 -0- 395 	 2808

JULY	STK B SOLD AT LOSS (10756 - 3015) NEW B SELL OCT CALLS OPTIONS SOLD AT 10 % OPTION PREM INCOME JUL	7561 -7956 795	7956 -0- 795	795
AUG	STK C CALLED OR EXPIRED STK C SELL NOV CALLS OPTIONS SOLD AT 10 % OPTION PREM INCOME AUG	10491 -11286 1128	11286 -0- 1128	1128
SEP	STK D SOLD AT LOSS (11295 - 3015) NEW D SELL DEC CALLS OPTIONS SOLD AT 10 % A&E CALLED OR EXPIRED STK A SELL DEC CALLS OPTIONS SOLD AT 10 % STK E SELL DEC CALLS OPTIONS SOLD AT 10 % NEW F SELL DEC CALLS OPTIONS SOLD AT 10 % OPTION PREM INCOME SEP	8280 -6706 670 16788 -10478 1048 -8584 858 -3004 300	9408 2702 3372 20160 9682 10730 2146 3004 -0- 300	2876
OCT	STK B CALLEDOR EXPIRED STK B SELL JAN CALLS OPTIONS SOLD AT 10 % OPTION PREM INCOME OCT	7957 -8257 826	8257 -0- 826	826
NOV	STK C CALLEDOR EXPIRED STK C SELL FEB CALLS OPTIONS SOLD AT 10 % OPTION PREM INCOME NOV	11286 -12112 1211	12112 -0- 1211	1211
DEC	A,D,E&F CALLED NEW A SELL MAR CALLS OPTIONS SOLD AT 10 % NEW D SELL MAR CALLS OPTIONS SOLD AT 10 % STK E SELL MAR CALLS OPTIONS SOLD AT 10 % STK F SELL MAR CALLS OPTIONS SOLD AT 10 % TAX RESERVE OPTION PREM INCOME DEC	28773 -11994 1199 -7676 768 -9825 982 -3438 343 3361	29984 17990 19190 11514 12282 2456 3438 -0- 343 -3018	3292
TOTAL PREMIUM INCOME YEAR THREE				**19470**

PORTFOLIO VALUE AT YEAR END		
		BALANCE
STOCK A	11994	11994
STOCK B	8257	20251
STOCK C	12112	32363
STOCK D	7676	40039
STOCK E	9825	49864
STOCK F	3438	53302
CASH	343	53645
25% TAX ON NET INCOME (PREMIUMS LESS LOSSES)	-3361	**50284**
ASSUMED STOCK LOSSES		6030
GAIN AFTER TAX & LOSS		10082
RETURN ON INVESTMENT		25.07%

"Here we are at the end of year three. As the portfolio has grown we have diversified. We began with only three stocks and now have six. Of course, in real life, further diversification is possible and desirable.

"In three years we have doubled our portfolio from $25,000 to $50,000. The compounding effect is just beginning to take effect. In another three years the portfolio can grow to $100,000. After 10 years we could grow the $25,000 to $250,000 based on our assumptions of 10% premium for three months, 25% tax and 15% stock market losses."

Louis Ruckhammer, the host and moderator, walked back on stage and shook hands with Rob as the audience burst into an appreciative round of applause.

"Professor, I have a few questions from the audience if you don't mind."

Rob nodded agreement.

"Question one: what about puts? The simulation only used covered calls."

"In my personal portfolio I use a strategy that combines calls and puts to optimize return. For the beginning options investor I strongly recommend sticking with covered calls until you have gained experience. I suppose you will have to invite me back on another cruise to learn my put strategy."

"We will," responded Louis. "Next question: For self directed IRA's and other retirement plans on which taxes are deferred, what would be the simulated result without taxes?

Rob quickly punched some numbers on his Illustrator and the number and the following table flashed on the screen.

"I have run the simulation with different factors. If you avoid tax, as with a retirement account, and all other factors are the same as the simulation we just demonstrated, then the $25,000 grows to $61,540 in three years. Here are some interesting scenarios, beginning with the one demonstrated in detail tonight:

COVERED CALL SIMULATION RESULTS						
Initial Invest.	Prem.	Cycle	Margin	Loss	Tax	3 YR Result
$25,000	10%	Quarterly	-0-	15%	25%	$50,284
$25,000	10%	Quarterly	-0-	15%	-0-	$61,540
$25,000	3%	Monthly	-0-	15%	-0-	$49,507
$25,000	4%	Monthly	40%	15%	25%	$73,406
$25,000	8%	Quarterly	40%	15%	25%	$48,965
$25,000	10%	Quarterly	40%	15%	25%	$62,861

"The premium percentage is the call option premium divided by its underlying stock cost for the cycle indicated. For the last three simulations using funds borrowed from the brokerage account an interest rate of 7% is factored in as an expense."

"Professor Graham, this has been a very illuminating presentation. We have one final question. Are you a bull or a bear with respect to the next few years?

Rob smiled. This was a question he could always expect. "I recently came across a chart that this group might find interesting. It's called 'Historical Buy & Sell Time Line' and goes from 1850 to 2018. I've been referring to it as the Cedric Chart because I learned about it from a newspaper column by Cedric Adams, a famous Minnesota newspaper columnist and radio personality very popular in the 1950's. Let's see if I can pull it up and flash it on the screen."

"Ah, here we go. I will leave it you to decide the predictive value of the chart. I have personally been impressed with how 'right on' the chart has been in prior years. If it is accurate we are in for five fat years, perhaps beginning sometime in or shortly after 2002."

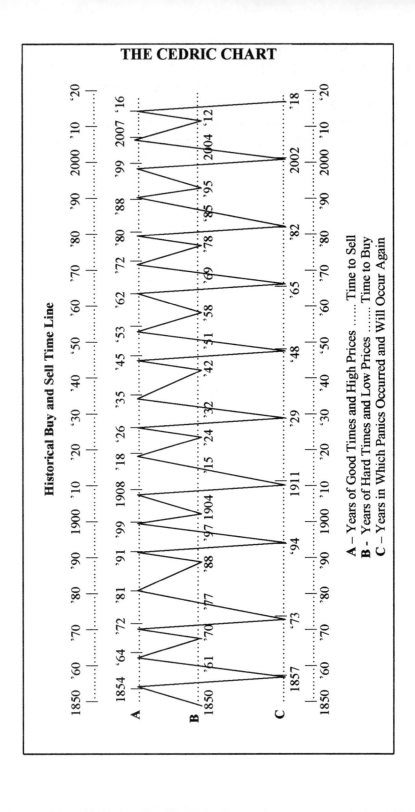

THE CEDRIC CHART

Historical Buy and Sell Time Line

A – Years of Good Times and High Prices ...... Time to Sell
B – Years of Hard Times and Low Prices ...... Time to Buy
C – Years in Which Panics Occurred and Will Occur Again

Louis Ruckhammer again broke in. "We have run out of time for additional questions. Thanks Rob for the wonderful insights into taking investment matters into our own hands. Maybe I can get you to visit me on my weekly TV show. If anyone else has a question for Rob and does not get it answered before the end of the cruise, he has agreed to accept questions at robgrahamphd@aol.com."

****

Later that evening Wayne and Sara invited Rob and Jean to join them on the balcony of their stateroom. Sara brought out mugs of decaf as they enjoyed the view of the full moon glistening on the Caribbean and reflected on the events of the past year.

Finally Wayne broached a subject that had been on his mind lately. "Professor, I believe I have mastered your strategy of stock selection and selling covered calls. We've done quite well this past year. Now....." There was a slight hesitation. "Now" he began again. "I think I'm ready for puts."

The professor thought for a moment as he took a sip of coffee. "Yes, Wayne. I do believe you are ready. With the expertise you have developed using covered calls you can benefit from the unique put strategy I have developed. You will also find it very rewarding.

GLOSSARY

American Stock Exchange (AMEX) - a private, not-for-profit corporation, located in New York City, that handles approximately one-fifth of all securities trades within the United States.

American Style Option - an option contract that can be exercised at any time between the date of purchase and the expiration date. The other type of contract is the European Style which may be exercised only during a specified period of time just prior to its expiration. Most exchange-traded options are American style.

Arbitrage - the simultaneous purchase and sale of identical financial instruments in order to make a profit where the selling price is higher than the buying price.

Arbitrageur - an individual that takes advantage of momentary disparities in prices between markets which enables one to lock in profits because the selling price is higher than the buying price.

Ask Price – the current cost to buy a security or option. It is the lowest price the seller will accept at that time.

At-The-Money – when an option's strike price is the same as the price of the underlying stock.

Automatic Exercise - the automatic exercise of an option that is in-the-money on expiration date.

Bear - an investor whose sentiment or belief is that a security or the market is falling or is expected to fall.

Bear Call Spread - a strategy in which a trader sells a lower strike call and buys a higher strike call to create a trade with limited profit and limited risk. A fall in the price of the underlying increases the value of the spread. This is a net credit transaction. The maximum loss is the difference between the strike prices less the credit. The maximum gain equals the credit.

Bear Market – the stock market cycle where prices for the overall market fall for an extended period of time usually caused by a weak economy and subsequent decreased corporate profits. It is generally agreed that a bear market is when the stock market experiences a price decline of twenty percent or more, and lasts at least two months.

Bear Put Spread - a strategy in which a trader sells a lower strike put and buys a higher strike put to create a trade with limited profit and limited risk. A fall in the price of the underlying increases the value of the spread. This is a net debit transaction. The maximum loss is the difference between the strike prices less the debit.

Bid Price – the current price you would receive if a stock (or option) is sold. It is the highest price the buyer will pay for that security at the present time.

Black Scholes Formula – a pricing model that is used by most options exchanges to price various options. It factors in the current stock price, strike price, time until expiration, current interest rates, and volatility of the underlying security.

Break-even – the price of an underlying security at which an option strategy neither gains nor loses money.

Bull - an investor whose sentiment or belief is that a security or the market is rising or is expected to rise.

Bull Market – the stock market cycle where prices for the overall market rise for an extended period of time usually caused by a strong economy and subsequent increased corporate profits.

Bull Call Spread - a strategy in which a trader buys a lower strike call and sells a higher strike call to create a trade with limited profit and limited risk. A rise in the price of the underlying increases the value of the spread. This is a net debit transaction. The maximum loss is equal to the debit. The maximum gain is the difference between the strike prices less the debit.

Bull Put Spread - a strategy in which a trader sells a higher strike put and buys a lower strike put to create a trade with limited profit and limited risk. A rise in the price of the underlying increases the value of the spread. This is a net credit transaction. The maximum loss is the difference between the strike prices less credit. The maximum gain is equal to the credit.

Buy Limit – the maximum price that should ever be paid for a stock, based on its 52 week low (L) and 52 week high (H).

$$\text{Buy Limit} = L + .25(H - L)$$

Buy Rank – a formula to rank the relative appeal of stocks on the prospect list. In the formula BL is Buy Limit, CP is current price, H is the 52 week high and L is the 52 week low.

$$\text{Buy Rank} = \frac{10(BL - CP)}{.25(H - L)}$$

Call Option – a contract that gives the holder the right (but not the obligation) to buy a specific stock at a predetermined price on or before a certain date (called the expiration date).

Chicago Board Options Exchange (CBOE) – the largest options exchange in the United States.

Covered Call – a short call option position against a long position in the underlying stock or index.

Covered Put - a short put option position against a short position in the underlying stock or index.

European Style Option - an option contract that may be exercised only during a specified period of time just prior to its expiration.

Exercise - implementing an option's right to buy or sell the underlying security.

Exercise Price – see strike price.

Expiration - the date and time after which an option may no longer be exercised.

Expiration Date - the last day on which an option may be exercised.

Fundamental Analysis – evaluating a company to determine if it is a good investment risk. Evaluation is based mainly on balance sheet and income statements, past records of earnings, sales, assets, management, products and services.

Go Long - to buy securities or options.

Good 'Till Canceled Order (GTC) - Sometimes simply called *GTC* it means an order to buy or sell stock that is good until you cancel it.

Go Short - to sell securities or options.

Holder - one who purchases an option.

Index - an index is a group of stocks which can be traded as one portfolio, such as the S&P 500. Broad-based indexes cover a wide range of industries and companies and narrow-based indexes cover stocks in one industry or economic sector.

Index Options - call and put options on indexes of stocks that allow investors to trade in a specific industry group or market without having to buy all the stocks individually.

In-the-Money – an option is In-the-Money to the extent it has intrinsic value. (See Intrinsic Value). A call option is said to be In-the-Money when the price of the underlying stock is higher than the strike price of the option. A put option is said to be In-the-Money when the price of the underlying stock is lower than the strike price of the option.

Intrinsic Value – a call option premium is said to have intrinsic value to the extent the stock price exceeds the strike price. A put option premium is said to have intrinsic value to the extent the strike price exceeds the stock price. The total value of the premium is intrinsic value (if any) plus the time value.

LEAPS (Long-term Equity AnticiPation Securities) – long dated options with expiration dates up to three years in the future.

Limit Order – a condition on a transaction to buy at or below a specified price or to sell at or above a specified price.

Long – a long position indicates that a stock, index, or option is owned.

Margin – a loan by a broker to allow an investor to buy more stocks or options than available money (cash) in the account.

Margin Requirements (Options) - the amount of cash an uncovered (naked) option writer is required to deposit and maintain to cover his daily position price changes.

Market Order – an order that is filled immediately upon reaching the trading floor at the next best available price.

NASDAQ (National Association of Securities Dealers Automated Quotations) - a computerized system providing brokers and dealers with price quotations for securities traded over-the-counter as well as for many New York Stock Exchange listed securities.

New York Stock Exchange (NYSE) - the largest stock exchange in the United States.

Option - a security that represents the right, but not the obligation, to buy or sell a specified amount of an underlying security (stock, bond, futures contract, etc.) at a specified price within a specified time.

Option Class – a group of calls or a group of puts on the same stock.

Option Holder - the buyer of either a call or put option.

Option Premium – the price it costs to buy an option or the price paid for selling an option.

Option Series – call or put options in the same class that have the same expiration date and strike price.

Option Writer - the seller of either a call or put option.

Out-of-the-Money - an option whose exercise price has no intrinsic value.

Out-of-the-Money Option (OTM) - a call option is out-of-the-money if its exercise or strike price is above the current market price of the underlying security. A put option is out-of-the-money if its exercise or strike price is below the current market price of the underlying security.

Premium – see Option Premium.

Price to Earnings Ratio (PE) – the current stock price divided by the earnings per share for the past year.

Put Option – a contract that gives the right (but not the obligation) to sell a specific stock at a predetermined price on or before a certain date (called the expiration date).

Security - a trading instrument such as stocks, bonds, and short-term investments.

Short – a short position indicates that a stock, index, or option is not owned.

Spread – the price gap between the bid and ask price of a stock.

Stock - a share of a company's stock translates into ownership of part of the company.

Stock Split - an increase in the number of a stock's shares with a corresponding decrease in the par value of its stock.

Straddle - a position consisting of a long call and a long put, or a short call and a short put, where both options have the same underlying security, strike price and expiration date.

Strangle - a position consisting of a long call and a long put or a short call and a short put, where both options have the same underlying security, the same expiration date, but different strike prices.

Strike Price – also called the exercise price, is the price at which a call option holder can purchase the underlying stock by exercising the option, and is the price at which a put option holder can sell the underlying stock by exercising the option.

TAI - Take Action Indicator. Formula for determining the relative attractiveness of stocks on the prospect list. In the formula BR is Buy Rank, FDA is Fifty Day Moving Average and CP is the current stock price.

$$TAI = BR \left(1 + \frac{FDA}{2(FDA) - CP} \right)$$

Technical Analysis - a method of evaluating securities and options by analyzing statistics generated by market activity, such as past high/low, up/down volume, momentum and moving averages.

Time Value – an option's premium consists of two parts: time value and intrinsic value. (See Intrinsic Value) The time value portion of the premium deteriorates with the passage of time and becomes zero with the expiration of the option.

Triple Witching Day - the third Friday in March, June, September and December when U.S. options, future options, and index options all expire on the same day.

Uncovered Call – a short call option in which the writer does not own the underlying security.

Uncovered Put – A short put option in which the writer does not have a corresponding short position on the underlying security.

Writer - an individual who sells an option

BOOK ORDER FORM

Mail this order form to:
Keller Publishing
590 Fieldstone Dr.
Marco Island, FL 34145

Fax this form to:
1-239-389-4307

Call Toll Free
1-800-631-1952

Order from web site
www.kellerpublishing.com

Ship to:

Name_____

Address_____

City_____

State/Zip_____

Phone_____

Email_____

Please send me the following copies of "The Money Tree"

Qty	Cost		Quantity			Total $
1-5	$19.95	X	_____	=	$	_____
6-25	$16.95	X	_____	=	$	_____
26-100	$13.95	X	_____	=	$	_____

Shipping & Handling

1-5--------------$4.95

6-25------------$8.95

26-100---------$12.95

S&H _____

FL Residents
add6%Tax _____

Total _____

METHOD OF PAYMENT

Check or money order payable to **Keller Publishing**

_____Visa _____MasterCard   Acct No:

Exp. date_____Signature_____

Thanks for your order. Please allow two weeks for delivery.

115

SOFTWARE ORDER FORM

Mail this order form to:

Keller Publishing
590 Fieldstone Dr.
Marco Island, FL 34145

Fax this form to:
1-239-389-4307

Call Toll Free
1-800-631-1952

Order from web site
www.kellerpublishing.com

Ship to:

Name_____

Address_____

City_____

State/Zip_____

Phone_____

Email_____

Please send me the following software programs:

The three software programs offered implement the concepts and techniques in *The Money Tree* for quick and easy application to your investment process.
_____CD or_____3.5 disc   Windows 95 and up

Item	Cost	Qty		Total $
OPTIONS SIMULATOR	$9.95	X ___ =	$	_____
CALL OPTION WIZARD	$9.95	X ___ =	$	_____
PROSPECT LIST MGR.	$9.95	X ___ =	$	_____
ALL THREE	$19.95	X ___ =	$	_____

OPTIONS SIMULATOR — As described in Chapter 10, generates expected return for any account size, level of margin, call premium values and monthly, quarterly or yearly option cycles.

CALL OPTION WIZARD — Computes the gain (if called or if expired) from call premiums on various strike prices and expiration dates. Indicates desirable (Magic Chart) premiums.

PROSPECT LIST MGR — Computes Buy Limit, Buy Rank & Take Action Indicator (TAI) for stocks on your prospect list. Also sort by any column.

$2.50 (S&H)

_____

6% FL Sales Tax
If Florida Resident

_____

TOTAL

Check or money order payable to **Keller Publishing**
_____Visa   _____MasterCard   Acct No:

Exp.date_____Signature_____

Thank you for your order.   Please allow two weeks for delivery.

BOOK ORDER FORM

Mail this order form to:
Keller Publishing
590 Fieldstone Dr.
Marco Island, FL 34145

Fax this form to:
1-239-389-4307

Call Toll Free
1-800-631-1952

Order from web site
www.kellerpublishing.com

Ship to:

Name_____

Address_____

City_____

State/Zip_____

Phone_____

Email_____

Please send me the following copies of "The Money Tree"

Qty	Cost		Quantity			Total $
1-5	$19.95	X	_____	=	$	_____
6-25	$16.95	X	_____	=	$	_____
26-100	$13.95	X	_____	=	$	_____

Shipping & Handling

1-5---------------$4.95

6-25-------------$8.95

26-100--------- $12.95

S&H _____

FL Residents
add6%Tax _____

Total _____

METHOD OF PAYMENT

Check or money order payable to **Keller Publishing**

_____Visa _____MasterCard   Acct No:

Exp. date_____Signature_____

Thanks for your order. Please allow two weeks for delivery.

SOFTWARE ORDER FORM

Mail this order form to:

Keller Publishing
590 Fieldstone Dr.
Marco Island, FL 34145

Fax this form to:
1-239-389-4307

Call Toll Free
1-800-631-1952

Order from web site
www.kellerpublishing.com

Ship to:

Name_____

Address_____

City_____

State/Zip_____

Phone_____

Email_____

Please send me the following software programs:

The three software programs offered implement the concepts and techniques in *The Money Tree* for quick and easy application to your investment process.

_____CD or_____3.5 disc   Windows 95 and up

Item	Cost	Qty		Total $
OPTIONS SIMULATOR	$9.95	X ___ =	$	_____
CALL OPTION WIZARD	$9.95	X ___ =	$	_____
PROSPECT LIST MGR.	$9.95	X ___ =	$	_____
ALL THREE	$19.95	X ___ =	$	_____

OPTIONS SIMULATOR — As described in Chapter 10, generates expected return for any account size, level of margin, call premium values and monthly, quarterly or yearly option cycles.

CALL OPTION WIZARD — Computes the gain (if called or if expired) from call premiums on various strike prices and expiration dates. Indicates desirable (Magic Chart) premiums.

PROSPECT LIST MGR — Computes Buy Limit, Buy Rank & Take Action Indicator (TAI) for stocks on your prospect list. Also sort by any column.

$2.50 (S&H)

_____

6% FL Sales Tax
If Florida Resident

_____

TOTAL

Check or money order payable to **Keller Publishing**
_____Visa   _____MasterCard   Acct No:

Exp.date_____Signature_____

Thank you for your order. Please allow two weeks for delivery.

.About the Authors

Ronald Groenke

Ron Groenke moved from Minnesota to the sunny gulf coast community of Marco Island after twenty-five years in the communications systems and software development environment. He has been active in the stock options market for fifteen years and developed the concepts and techniques provided in the book. On Marco, he and wife, Jean, are active in their church and busy entertaining family and friends who visit from the north.

Besides options investing/advising, other activities include personal computing, Rotary, walking, boating, and traveling.

Ron can be reached at robgrahamphd@aol.com

Wade Keller

Wade Keller, a native of Greenville, Georgia, has retired from careers as Owner/Manager of a CPA Firm and College Professor. Currently he is a writer, primarily a ghost writer of personal memoirs.

Wade and wife, Sue, live on Marco Island, Florida where a main activity is spending time with their five grandchildren, ages one to thirteen.

Other than writing and grandkids, interests include, Toastmasters, Rotary, chess, reading, travel, national politics, and walking on the beach at sunset with Sue. The couple has recently learned the rewards of writing covered calls.

Wade can be reached at wade@marcocondo.com